Suddenly an NVA in khaki uniform walks out of a bunker hidden under one of the hooches. As he steps into daylight, he sees a line of Marines walking about thirty feet away on the retaining wall. He draws a 9mm pistol from his belt and shoots a Marine, center chest, through an open flak jacket. . . .

We hear the shooting and see the line of Marines drop down behind the low wall. Immediately a fight breaks out between the Marines there and an undetermined number of enemy hidden in and around the hooches.

Before we can react to the action, we take automatic fire from somewhere behind and below us. We all hit the deck, but because we are up on the side of the hill, our profiles are still visible even when we lie down. The firing at us continues. Several weapons are shooting at once, and bullets are flying all around. Every good war story has the same incident: The men on either side of me are hit. The Marine on my right takes a bullet through the left arm. The Marine on my left gets hit in the right thigh. And the shooting continues.

We cannot stay put, but there is no place to go. If something doesn't happen quickly, we will take a lot of casualties.

DOWN SOUTH
One Tour in
Vietnam

William H. Hardwick

PRESIDIO PRESS

BALLANTINE BOOKS • NEW YORK

A Presidio Press Book
Published by The Random House Publishing Group
Copyright © 2004 by William H. Hardwick

All rights reserved under International and Pan-American Copyright Conventions. Published in the United States by The Random House Publishing Group, a division of Random House, Inc., New York, and simultaneously in Canada by Random House of Canada Limited, Toronto.

Presidio Press and colophon are registered trademarks of Random House, Inc.

Grateful acknowledgment is made for permission to reprint previously published material:

Spinning Wheel
Words and Music by David Clayton Thomas
© 1968 (Renewed 1996) EMI BLACKWOOD MUSIC INC. and BAY MUSIC LTD.
All Rights Controlled and Administered by EMI BLACKWOOD MUSIC INC.
All Rights Reserved. International Copyright Secured. Used by Permission.

And When I Die
Words and Music by Laura Nyro
© 1966 (Renewed 1994) EMI BLACKWOOD MUSIC INC.
All Rights Reserved. International Copyright Secured. Used by Permission.

www.presidiopress.com

ISBN 0-89141-847-4

Manufactured in the United States of America

First Edition: August 2004

OPM 10 9 8 7 6 5 4 3 2 1

To Dixie, for your love, your trust, and your faith.
The best thing that ever happened to me.

Contents

Preface

In my time I have loved the Marine Corps, hated the Marine Corps, and loved it again. I have always been intensely proud of the Marines with whom I served, and I have always been intensely proud of my service as a Marine. When I first returned from Vietnam, I had strong feelings of betrayal. I was angry and bitter at what I thought the Marine Corps had "done" to the Americans who were either killed or maimed while keeping the faith. Over time I began to realize that the Corps was just doing what it does, what it must be able to do.

Marines are America's shock troops. Time and again, the Corps was given the worst and dirtiest jobs that our country had to face. And time and again, Marines found a way to get the job done. From Belleau Wood to Iwo Jima to Inchon, the Marine Corps has been America's ace in the hole. A Marine rifle company in an assault is both terrible and magnificent in its violence—a real-life terminator.

Hindsight is always better, and after more than thirty years, so many things seem so much clearer. Yet historians argue about the lessons learned from the Vietnam

War. At the time we had a long list of similarities between the Korean and Vietnamese conflicts. In 1965 it very much appeared that twenty years of Cold War struggle and the policy of containment had "stopped the spread" of communism. So it only made sense to continue this successful policy in Vietnam. Barely ten years after the McCarthy hearings and the Korean cease-fire, if South Vietnam had fallen without some kind of fight, someone would have suffered some very negative political consequences. Perhaps we should have paid less attention to the similarities between Korea and Vietnam and more attention to their differences.

Korea is a peninsula. We could seal and control three of the country's four borders, and no organized indigenous guerrilla movement existed in South Korea. Vietnam on the other hand has a long, difficult land border, and its guerrillas had been organizing, training, and permeating the community for years before Americans arrived. The problems faced in Vietnam are more similar to the problems we face today in trying to stop the flow of drugs into the United States. Perhaps the Marine Corps—or any conventional military force—was the wrong tool for the job, or perhaps we were doing the wrong job.

When I came back from Vietnam, all I wanted to do was forget the experience. I could not watch the news; I knew what was going to happen and I could not bear it. Even though it was on my mind almost every day, for the first ten years after I returned I just tried to not think about it. But after more than thirty years, I found that I really was forgetting. Now, as if losing an old friend, I want to save it.

In order to write this story, I had to go back and relive

it. Some of this was very difficult to relive. Although what I describe here is such a small part of what happened, like seeing the war through a peephole, after all these years this is all that's left.

I joined the Marine Corps partly for something exciting to do, partly because I believed in fighting communism, and partly to prove to myself that I was as good or as worthy as the previous generation of Americans. If my country was in a fight, I thought that it was my duty to go. Faced with the same decision today, I would do the same thing. I cannot give you any great personal insight from my experience in Vietnam, but if there is a history lesson here, then I give this to you.

Semper Fidelis!

January 2004

Acknowledgments

Writing this story has been an interesting journey. This effort began as a mental health exercise and eventually took on a life of its own. Along the way many people have become a part of this writing, and I would not have finished without them.

My family, of course, has supported this and enabled me to get it down on paper the first time. I have dedicated the book to my wife, Dixie. My daughters, Christin and Kelly, still think I am a hero.

When I thought the story was clear enough to understand, I sent a copy to the Vietnam Archives at Texas Tech University in Lubbock, Texas. Not long afterward, Dr. James Reckner, the head of Texas Tech's history department, called to say hello. He encouraged me to seek a publisher. He has been a catalyst in this; my deepest thanks to him.

With regard to editing and wisdom, Eric Hammell has carried the load. There is no substitute for experience and Eric has been a great point man.

I "finished" this story the first time in 1996. Over the next three or four years I would go back, a little at a time, and fill in, or explain better. It started as a connect-the-dots exercise and slowly grew into a full story. It was finally the men of Mike 3/7 and Bravo 1/5 who filled in so many gaps and really completed the picture.

I had the two best company commanders in any war. Col. Gene (Gino) Castagnetti is as tough, as smart, and as dedicated as any man he ever served with or fought against. The man earned his pay every day. His professional knowledge, his personal courage, and his unwavering dedication to his job and his troops got many Marines home alive, including me.

Lt. Gen. Paul K. Van Riper's career as a Marine speaks for itself. He was everything you could hope for in a commanding officer. He kept me alive and taught me how to fight.

The backbone of any organization is its middle management. In the thirty-plus years I have been out of the Marines, I have not found any organization with a middle management that was as high-quality as that of the United States Marine Corps. NCOs in the Marine Corps may not be perfect, but if professionalism and effectiveness count, they would rate at the top of any *Fortune* 500 survey. Richard Gregory and Donald Henderson would set the standard. "Yea, if I must walk through the valley, let me take the gunny with me."

To all the guys who have taken an interest in this story, thank you. To the friends I know best—John Juracek, Gene Gray, Terry Williamson, Lou Piatt, John Mason, Lee Neely, Tom Harrell—I am glad that, one way or another, we all made it back. I know that none of us will ever forget the guys who didn't.

Thanks to the grunts who really did the fighting; unless you have tasted it and smelled it and *been* it, you will never understand what combat really is. In the final analysis, it is the fighting spirit of the grunts that must carry the day. I am proud and honored to have served with the Americans who were Marines in Vietnam. We fought hard. I am still in awe of the daily courage that I witnessed.

A special word of gratitude to David Bruneau and Maxey Gilleland from Mike 3/7, and John Wheeler, David Marks, and Greg Kraljev from Bravo 1/5. I barely knew these guys while I was there. Like so many others, they were tough, smart Marines, and it was not until later that I came to appreciate how good they really are.

Last but far from least, thanks to my new best friend, Bruce Cader. Bruce was a machine gunner in Bravo 1/5. He is a Marine through and through. When he says, "I loved the Marine Corps more than life itself," Bruce means it. We stood side by side through some of the toughest times I have ever seen and we never got to know each other. If I had known at the time that we were both going to make it home alive, I would have been friendlier.

There are more than fifty-eight thousand names on the Vietnam Wall. Let us never forget their sacrifice. There are several times that number of Americans who came home with either physical or emotional wounds. Those veterans have to deal with problems every day that we cannot heal and sometimes can't even understand. Let us never forget the sacrifice that they continue to make.

Glossary

0300   military occupational specialty: infantry officer

0800   military occupational specialty: artillery officer

air panel   Red-and-yellow three-foot-square plastic cloth set out by infantry to indicate their position to aircraft

AO   aerial observer (for artillery)

APC   armored personnel carrier

ARVN   Army of the Republic of (South) Vietnam

dustoff   medevac helicopter

E-tool   entrenching tool; a small folding shovel

FAC   forward air controller

FDC   fire direction center

flechette   type of antipersonnel ammunition filled with small steel darts

FO   forward observer (for artillery)

FSC   fire support coordinator

gunny   gunnery sergeant; chief NCO in a rifle platoon

HE   high explosive

LZ   landing zone (for helicopters)

MAD   mutual assured destruction

medevac   medical evacuation (by helicopter)

MOS   military occupational specialty

NCO   noncommissioned officer

OCS   officer candidate school

ROTC   Reserve Officer Training Corps

skipper   rifle company commander

snuffy   enlisted personnel; private through sergeant (E1–E4)

TAOR   tactical area of responsibility

WP   Willie Pete: white phosphorus ammunition used to mark targets

XO   executive officer

One More for the Corps

I will not be the first American president to lose a war.
—RICHARD M. NIXON, 1969

By the mid-1960s it was clear that political stability
did not exist and was unlikely ever to be achieved . . .
the South Vietnamese, even with our training assis-
tance and logistical support, were incapable of defend-
ing themselves. . . . I deeply regret that I did not force
a probing debate about whether it would ever be possible to forge a winning military effort on a foundation of
political quicksand. It became clear then, and I believe
it is clear today, that military force—especially when
wielded by an outside power—cannot bring order in a
country that cannot govern itself.
—ROBERT MCNAMARA, APRIL 1995

September 27, 1968. We were ten Marine second lieutenants in a commercial airliner jammed full of Marine
and navy personnel, all headed from Okinawa to Da
Nang. Since 1961 the war in Vietnam had grown from
something approximating a civil defense drill using
American advisers to a full-blown American war in
Asia. By this date, five hundred thousand American
troops were involved, and the fighting was raging. My
twenty-fourth birthday was less than a month away.

In December 1966, I was a senior at the University of
Oklahoma when I signed on for Marine Corps OCS (officer candidate school). The war then was still relatively
small. American forces were suffering about fifty killed

per week. At that time, three hundred thousand Americans were in Vietnam. I knew that going there would be dangerous, but the danger seemed to make this grand adventure even more alluring.

I joined the Marines with my eyes open. Growing up right after World War II and during the Korean War, I had read war novels and chronicles. After participating in ROTC (Reserve Officer Training Corps) for three years in high school, I knew what I was getting into. In spite of that, or perhaps because of it, I still wanted to be in a firefight. I wanted to see how I would respond. The war in Vietnam seemed like an opportunity to fight communism and have a great story to tell my grandchildren. Along the way, however, something went terribly wrong.

In January 1968, while I was still training at Quantico, Virginia, completing my officer's basic training, the communists launched their Tet Offensive. The number of Americans killed each week jumped from fifty to five hundred. Although the Tet Offensive turned into a military defeat for the communists, the shock of the event shattered American resolve. Mike Thomas, a fraternity brother of mine, died in the fighting around Hue during the first week of Tet. Mike had "caught one between the running lights" (between the eyes), I was told. The war was turning into a giant meat grinder. As the war raged in Southeast Asia, the antiwar movement was also raging back in the States.

The year 1968 was big for shocking events. In February, Lyndon Johnson announced that he would not seek reelection. In April, Martin Luther King, Jr., was assassinated in Memphis, and in June, Bobby Kennedy was assassinated in California. In August, at the Democratic National Convention in Chicago, antiwar demonstrators gathered from around the country, and Mayor Richard Daly's police force waged a running, screaming, club-swinging battle that was broadcast nationwide on television. The spectacle divided the country like no event had since the Civil War.

As a result, the nation turned its collective back on Vietnam. You can go into the magazine stacks in the library and look up the old *Time* magazines. In 1961, Vietnam was an occasionally mentioned subject in the Foreign Affairs box. By Christmas 1967 through March 1968, Vietnam almost dominated the magazine. Nine months later, by Christmas 1968, the subject had returned to the Foreign Affairs box. Yet the fighting continued for another four years. Only the events at Kent State would shock the nation enough to refocus on the war. From 1969 through 1972, 20,400 Americans died in the war. Thousands upon thousands of young Americans were maimed, physically or emotionally, for life.

I suppose no one in the chain of command had stopped to consider what it would mean, in a democracy, to use American draftees to fight a war of attrition in Asia.

Even as our airliner descended toward the beginning of our thirteen-month-long tours, Richard Nixon was successfully campaigning across the country with his "secret plan" to end the fighting and bring the troops home. Everyone on the plane expected our tours to be cut short; no one wanted to be the last American killed in Vietnam. But during that Cold War time, Americans were having to choose. If my country was in a fight, I wanted to be there, so I signed up.

Our class of 240 new second lieutenants graduated from the Basic School (TBS) in May 1968. After a twenty-day leave, the eighty infantry officers (military occupational specialty 0300) had gone directly to Vietnam. The rest of us broke up to attend different schools in other specialties. Fifty of us reported to artillery school for three months at Fort Sill in Lawton, Oklahoma, in order to become artillery officers, or "cannon-cockers" (MOS 0800).

Word came almost immediately that two of our classmates had been killed in combat. One had graduated second-in-class. Both were blown in half by enemy land mines made from American artillery rounds. Neither man survived his first week.

The news hit Fort Sill like a bomb. For the next three months we would periodically hear the name of another classmate dead or wounded. It had the feel of a real war. The day we graduated from artillery school, ten of us were diverted one more time. We were assigned to Coronado Naval Air Station, south of San Diego, for four weeks. There we were crosstrained as forward air controllers (FACs) in a Marine Corps experiment to see if artillery officers could do the combat air controller's job, thereby eliminating the need to risk expensively trained pilots. It gave me a warm feeling to know where I fell on the Defense Department's list of expendables.

As we headed toward Da Nang, the mood and temperament in America were changing. We had no way of knowing this at the time (and would receive precious little real news for the next thirteen months), but all through 1968 and 1969, this was the case. As we began our tours, the rules and even reality itself were changing back in "the World." We would all go home to a different nation.

In Okinawa, Vietnam was referred to as "down south." The words were spoken with a certain reverence that expressed both excitement and dread, and they sounded ominous to me. In 1968, down south was a bad place to be.

We were new Marines, and although we were anxious and afraid, we were itching to fight. We had been in training for a full year, and now we were headed to war. I must admit that the spike in violence brought on by the Tet Offensive had scared all of us. We were aware that the war was growing more unpopular, but this was an idea that I rejected. I think the ten of us really believed America could win, that somehow America *would* win.

In Okinawa the dominant theme was, "It's not a very big war, but it's the only war we have." The ten of us were headed, one step at a time, toward the war. Each of us was going to discover how bad it could be down south.

Vietnam is beautiful; there is no other way to describe it. As we flew in, we peered down at the crystal water, bleached white beaches, the flat plains, and the thickly overgrown green mountain ranges below—simply beautiful. While our airliner descended into the airspace over Vietnam, we watched through the windows as two fighter aircraft made looping dives down through the atmosphere at an unseen target. Somewhere on the ground, amidst all the foliage, a FAC was watching from a very different perspective. It was both exciting and frightening.

Soon after we landed, five of us were assigned to 1st Marine Division, headquartered in Da Nang. The other five were flown north to 3d Marine Division. Of us five remaining in Da Nang, I knew John Juracek and Jim Harvey the best. The three of us had been together since OCS. Now, as the five of us were about to split up for new assignments, we wondered aloud if we would meet here again on our way back home. Back in the World it had been a crazy year, perhaps a direct result of the even crazier world we were entering.

At the time I was fully in favor of the war. I believed in the Domino Theory—that if Vietnam fell, then Cambodia, Laos, and Thailand would fall to the communists. Therefore, under the Hegemony Theory, all of Asia would fall into the hands of Mao Tse-tung and the communist Chinese. On the other hand, we had the "MAD theory"—mutual assured destruction. The Cold War generated a lot of mad theories. It turned out that all we had to do to defeat communism was to let it succeed. It just took another twenty years for that to happen.

1st Marine Division headquarters was built into the backside (ocean side) of the mountains overlooking Da Nang. That configuration kept HQ from being hit directly by rockets. But being in the shade of the mountain also gave me a strange sensation. That first night, several of us sat on the deck outside the officers club and watched a small firefight. It was to our north, perhaps fifteen hundred meters away, but because it happened on the mountainside directly in front of us, the flashes, crackling rifle fire, and sharp explosions had a thrilling, chilling effect.

Some officers in our group who knew the company commander involved in the fight laughed at his luck. He was nearing the end of his tour and had been brought back to perimeter defense in Da Nang because it was quiet and safe. As it turned out, this was the third night of the last five that his company had been in contact. As I sat on that deck watching and listening to a real fire-fight, reality seemed to take on a sharper focus.

The war seemed immense. It was happening in the air, on the ground, and all around. It created its own atmosphere in which extreme violence was normal. It seemed to me that we were at the edge of that atmosphere and looking in. Tomorrow the five of us would begin our separate journeys, and although I was not feeling especially fatalistic, I could not escape feeling the enormity of the war; it seemed so awesome.

The Marine Corps and indeed every Marine has one primary responsibility: accomplish the mission. In Vietnam, the Corps' mission was "to close with and kill the enemy." Tomorrow we would begin living in a very different world, and I was excited and more than a little anxious.

The next morning, just before noon, we were summoned to the division commander's office. It was a metal shell covered with sandbags. Fifteen or so NCOs (noncommissioned officers) and field-grade officers also met the general. His office was a big room with a low ceiling. On one side was a large desk with battle flags behind it. The other side was an open area for gatherings such as this. The general, gray and balding, was a kindly man whose attitude toward us was more like a grandfather's than a Marine division commander's.

The general welcomed us to 1st Marine Division and used a large map to give us a brief update on the action around the division's tactical area of responsibility (TAOR). We all stood in a circle with the general in the middle as he chatted briefly with a major and first sergeant he knew. Then he turned in our direction and said, "You are headed to 11th Marines to become forward observers. Right now the Marine Corps has a desperate shortage of platoon commanders. We have many platoons being led by staff sergeants and sergeants. This is an opportunity for some of you, or all of you, to step forward and take a platoon. The Marine Corps is counting on you."

Suddenly the room fell breathless. Each of us wanted a platoon, but we also knew the terrible reason behind the Marine Corps' "desperate shortage" of platoon commanders. America was about to pull out of Vietnam. I, for one, had made my pact. I would obey every order and do my job to the best of my ability. If that got me killed, so be it. Otherwise, I would keep my head down and try to get myself and every other American home alive. The general's offer was a real surprise, but as the room waited and the war grew older, five gold bars stood frozen in place. My breath was trapped in my throat, and the only sound in the room was the ticking clock on the general's desk. My eyes were straight ahead, staring at a spot on the far wall.

After a long ten seconds the general spoke again: "Well, then. I want to welcome each of you again to 1st Division, and best of luck to each of you on your tours. That is all." The other officers and NCOs at the gathering, all "lifers" on their second or third tours, filed casually out of the office with bemused smiles on their faces. The five second lieutenants marched stone-faced from the general's office, still without breathing. This is not a hero's story.

From 1st Division headquarters we rode down the hill

two hundred meters to 11th Marines headquarters. The 11th Marine Regiment provided artillery support for all of 1st Marine Division. Each of us was assigned to a 105mm howitzer battery (six cannons) in support of a rifle battalion (four infantry companies). From there, each battery would attach us to one of its rifle companies as a forward observer (FO) for the guns. My job would be to provide my infantry company with close artillery support. I was assigned to India Battery, 3/11 (3d Battalion, 11th Marine Regiment), in support of 3d Battalion, 7th Marine Regiment. I was issued jungle utilities (trousers and a long-sleeved shirt), jungle boots, a steel helmet, a flak jacket, a .45-caliber service automatic with holster, two magazines, and a cartridge belt. The supply clerk then told me where to catch the next armored convoy to India Battery.

Armored convoys usually had one tank at the front and another at the rear. Between them would be anywhere from ten or fifteen to forty or fifty trucks, jeeps, weapons, and pieces of equipment. Except during Tet, when they shot at everything, the enemy seldom messed with these convoys. I would soon discover that going anywhere in a convoy was a real pain. Convoys were dirty, hot, and for the most part boring, but that morning it did not matter. I was "in-country" and headed out to "Indian country," and I was very excited. I was ready bright and early. Wearing my brand-new jungle fatigues and boots, I almost skipped over to the truck rendezvous point. We covered the twenty-five miles to Hill 37 and India Battery in about six hours.

North of Da Nang, the mountains jut right up to the coast. But to the south and west of Da Nang, the mountains have been carved away over the ages by several rivers that created valleys. Spreading out from west to east, these valleys start as narrow openings in mountains that run up to thirty-five hundred feet. The valleys slowly widen as the rivers meander toward the coast. Several miles from the coast, it all goes flat. Hill 37 is one of the three or four hills that command a view over one of these valleys; it sits almost in the center of the valley, which at that location is four to five miles wide. The road came in from the north and the river ran along the south. From Hill 37 the river ran east past Hill 55 and through the South Koreans' TAOR to the ocean. I spent two days at India Battery becoming familiar with the guns, the charts, and the first sensations of being at war. I had a kind of naked feeling.

In Vietnam, everyone was in the same boat, and everyone tried to help each other with good advice. For two days I took in so much information that my mind began to overload. Artillery batteries in Vietnam shot around the clock and around the compass. The battery commander was careful to warn me, "Don't ever shoot 105s with troops short on the gun-target line." The barrel on a 105 has a service life of seven thousand rounds. India Battery was firing a thousand rounds per day, so the life of all the barrels could not run much longer than forty-two days. But this is the Marine Corps, and not only had India been firing at that rate for ten months, the battery commander swore the tubes were at least seventeen years old and had fought in Korea.

A battery of six cannons comprises three platoons of two guns each. In Vietnam most fire missions were fired by a platoon. It was not uncommon to have one platoon firing in one direction while another platoon fired in a different direction in support of a different unit. And of course, every battery was open for business twenty-four hours of every day. The crews often slept with the guns, if they slept at all, and at times the firing got fast and furious.

Crews worked hard. When they weren't shooting during the daytime, they worked on the guns, worked on the defenses, and often went on patrols. Every Marine is a rifleman first. When the artillerymen weren't shooting at night, they stood watch in the lines or sat out in ambushes or listening posts.

The Marine Corps invented the term "close coordinated supporting fires." In Vietnam our support was layered. The grunts carried 60mm mortars that were effective out to seventeen hundred meters. They also had 81mm mortars, effective out to forty-eight hundred meters. Next came the 105mm howitzer, which can shoot effectively out to eleven thousand meters. The big cannons—the 155mm howitzers, the 8-inch howitzers, and the 175mm guns—will shoot farther than you could care about. Of course, on top of all that we had "the Wing." The 1st Marine Air Wing may catch a lot of grief from the rest of the Corps, but no one else in the world can provide the kind of close support that the Wing can. When the Wing arrives, the battle turns. You can count on it.

Even with all of that, there were huge holes in our coverage. The enemy was usually elusive, and as a result we were constantly moving weapons and troops. Given our tremendous advantage in firepower, we were able to stay spread out in small units. The war was an enormous operation.

Cannon crews are teams, and no one does teamwork better than the Marine Corps. A good FO "in contact" could have the "05s" up and cranking in three minutes or less. Quick, accurate fire from 105s was usually the first help an infantry unit could count on. The crews worked hard and fought hard, but inevitably there were mistakes. In Vietnam there were a lot of mistakes.

India Battery was lovingly referred to as Idiot Battery. It seems that on one unfortunate day they shot five guns west and one gun east, 180 degrees out, hitting the back of the mess hall on Hill 55. No one was seriously hurt, but it broke all the dishes, and regimental headquarters personnel had to eat out of their mess kits for several days.

On October 3 the battery commander drove me to my new assignment as FO for Mike Company, 3d Battalion, 7th Marines (3/7). Mike Company was headquartered on Hill 55, about ten thousand meters (six miles) east of Hill 37. The river flowed past Hill 55, and Mike Company had security for the bridge nicknamed Golden Gate. The CO (commanding officer), Capt. Paul Van Riper, had a twin brother who was also a Marine captain. Van Riper was now on his second tour. On his first tour, as a platoon commander, he won a Silver Star, took a bullet in the left side, and ultimately lost his spleen. The twin brothers had a reputation at Basic School in Quantico for chewing up new second lieutenants in bunches. Paul Van Riper was thin and about six feet three inches tall. He wore wire-rim glasses, was careful and thoughtful, and at age twenty-nine his crew cut was beginning to show gray. He seldom spoke loudly, and you might take him to be a mild-mannered college professor, but you would be making a mistake. I quickly found out that Paul Van Riper was the best friend a new second lieutenant in Vietnam could have. He kept me alive.

In a Marine Corps rifle company, the company commander is referred to as "the skipper." In Vietnam, most of the first sergeants were detached to battalion HQ or regiment in order to keep the paperwork flowing. The chief operational NCO for the Marine rifle company is the gunnery sergeant, "the gunny." In the most autocratic organization still functioning today, a rifle company is democratic in at least one way: Every morning each man stuffs all his current possessions into his pack, then he swings that pack up on his back, and off you all hump.

Mike Company was stationed on Hill 55 and had twelve-man tents with wood floors made from pallets and plywood. Because Hill 55 was also the regimental HQ for 7th Marines, there was a mess hall where they showed movies at night and a staff club where you could find whiskey and cold beer, and of course, a most precious commodity in Vietnam, ice.

Mike Company's TAOR included Golden Gate Bridge and the area across the river several thousand meters south. Mike patrolled its TAOR with small units: platoons, squads, or sometimes three-man units. Some went out in the morning and came in before dark, and some went out in the afternoon and came in the next morning, but most patrols lasted fewer than twenty-four hours. Patrols followed a predetermined course that changed each day. Much of this activity came right out of the *Small Unit Tactics* manual. At dark, everyone who was out set up an ambush. Usually, once or twice during the night they would move the ambush. Moving at night in Vietnam was always dangerous. If you were down and still at night, you were almost invisible and almost invulnerable. When you moved around at night you became very vulnerable. It was dangerous to create a "skyline" or silhouette.

The Marines in Mike Company were aggressive. The attitude I heard expressed more than once was, "Fuck this waiting around, let's go pick a fight." Most of the Marines were very good at it and many of them liked it. I can tell you that war can be very attractive, even addictive. In 1968, I had never heard of endorphins, but I could have told you then that there is something about the human body that gets a tremendous "thrill" from combat. It can be a nervous time, constantly looking for a fight. Finding a firefight can be terrifying for a brief moment or for as long as it lasts. As soon as it is over and the looking begins again, you may notice a desire or yearning for more. The absence of fear can make you feel hollow.

I had been with Mike Company for only two days when word came down for us to pack up and move out. We would take an armored convoy out to Hill 52. At Hill 55 we were located about ten kilometers east of Hill 37 and India Battery. The move would put us about ten kilometers west of their position. Several artillery pieces were moving out to Hill 52 to support a new operation named Maui Peak.

Mike Company and others would spend three weeks on Hill 52, doubtless with some action but mostly just in hill defense. When we arrived we found that we had a platoon of 155mm self-propelled howitzers and a platoon of 8-inch self-propelled howitzers, lovingly referred to as "hogs," stationed on the hill. Most of the big guns like these were self-propelled. Two or three tanks were attached to plug any holes in the line. We had to be watchful when the tanks fired. Overpressure from the muzzle blast can kill or badly injure anyone standing too close to the muzzle. We heard stories about Marines bleeding from the nose or ears after being too close to a firing tank, so I always gave the tanks plenty of room.

Mike Company had defense of the eastern and northern sides of Hill 52. The river snakes out of the mountains from the west, passes south of the hill, and winds its way east past Hill 37 and out to the coast. Visibility east was open and almost unlimited. One thousand meters south across the river was a high ridge that we controlled. To the west we could see about fifteen hundred meters of river before it disappeared into the mountains. To the north four thousand meters away, across broken terrain with rice paddies, tree lines, and rough ground, was Charlie Ridge. Several old-timers told me it was appropriately named. Charlie Ridge was a long, high hogback, covered with solid vegetation, that jutted several hundred feet above Hill 52. A few months back, Mike Company and the rest of 3/7 along with two other battalions had been up on Charlie Ridge and cleared it of many—I won't say all—enemy soldiers. Hill 52 had been vacant since. The engineers swept the hill for mines and booby traps before we arrived, and we settled in to do our small part in Operation Maui Peak.

Company headquarters was a sandbagged circle on top of the hill. A ship's glass mounted on a tripod gave us a good look at the ridge, the paddies, and the surrounding terrain. The company's routine during the day was to have two platoons on patrol and one on the hill. At night, all three platoons filled the lines, and each sent out patrols or ambushes. My days were filled with teaching grunts how to call in fire missions, improving my fighting hole, or getting caught up in some project Gunny Gregory had. But mostly I watched for targets. The best time to look for targets was early morning and late afternoon, just like hunting game.

Most of the daytime patrols found nothing. Some of the nighttime patrols made contact. One night, during a two-hour moving gunfight, one patrol killed at least two NVA (North Vietnamese Army) soldiers and found blood and drag marks that indicated several more had been killed or wounded.

Maui Peak lasted three weeks, and I went out on only three or four patrols. The skipper kept reminding me that I could see much better from on top of the hill. But I was feeling good about all this. I liked the excitement, I was learning my job, and I wanted some action.

It goes without saying that it was hot. Hot and dirty. Hill 52 had long since given up all vegetation, and when the weather was dry, it was just a tall, hot mound of dirt. When the weather was wet, it was a miserable, sloppy mess. It rained a lot while we were there.

A number of events stick in my mind. We had been there about a week, and I was standing at the ship's glass, looking at Charlie Ridge for the one hundredth time, when I heard a loud *crunch* overhead. When I looked up I saw that two helicopters, one a CH-46 taking off and one a CH-34 landing, had collided about five hundred feet in the air just east of the hill. The two ships seemed to weld together, frozen in space for a moment. Then a fire sparked, a very bright fire that burned like a Fourth of July sparkler. The pair of tangled choppers went through a slow, spiraling descent. The fall lasted only seconds, but the fire burned so intensely that when they finally crashed in the river bottom, they hit not with a *thump* but with a *whoosh*. Marines rushed to the site, but we all knew no one could have survived. Someone later told me that the skin of a CH-34 was made of magnesium and that is why it sparkled when it burned. The fire was so hot that it melted the barrel on one of the .50-caliber waist guns. Fifteen Marines died in about fifteen seconds.

The artillery pieces shot from time to time, but the guns were certainly not overused. One afternoon we were standing up on the hill when off in the distance to our west we heard a burst from a machine gun, then some shouting. Looking west at the river through the ship's glass, I could see a wooden sampan with what appeared to be two people aboard headed downstream toward us about a thousand meters away. The skipper was calling for a tank to move across the hill and down the slope to a clear firing position, but before anyone could move, the captain commanding the self-propelled 155s jumped on the back of one of the howitzers and had the driver backing up and traversing toward the river. They had a clear firing position, but I would not have given you a nickel for their chances of being effective. Still, with a 155mm round, all he had to do was get close.

When he had the barrel lined up on the river, the captain opened the breech and looked through the barrel to direct-sight the river for elevation. The whole exercise took less than a minute. He had the crew seat a round and the full three charges (cannons always fire full charge—maximum charge—when firing direct fire). The captain checked his alignment again and waited a few more seconds for the sampan to near a bend where the river turns slightly south.

We were standing behind and just to the left of the gun when it fired. From that location we could see the projectile leave the muzzle and then disappear on its way. We later estimated that the boat was about eight hundred meters out, and all eyes were on the sampan as the big howitzer recoiled. Two seconds later the sampan disappeared.

I saw some great shots in Vietnam, but this had to be the most spectacular. There was the flash that you get with a direct hit, and then the detonation obscured vision for a split second. When the smoke cleared, there was nothing. There were no pieces splashing in the water, no debris floating downstream, there was nothing. I suppose "vaporize" may be too strong a term, but as the black smoke dissipated, we looked through binoculars and the ship's glass, and the water was clear and clean. Cheers and applause broke out up and down the hill, as did a kind of low, whispered "Wowee." That captain gained great face around the battalion. For days, Marines would wander past the howitzers just to see them operate, as though they might be magic.

A couple of days later, just after first light, we were looking up at Charlie Ridge through the glass when we saw a shirtless NVA soldier standing in front of a cave entrance, shaving. A moment later he was joined by another NVA in uniform holding something in his hand, perhaps tea. The 8-inch howitzers were right in front of us, beginning their day. Inspired by the show the 155s had provided, I called down to the captain in command. He trotted up to the glass and peered through. His eyes lit up and he scrambled back down to his hogs, shouting instructions and looking at his map for distance.

In all fairness to the 8-inch gun crew, this was a much more difficult shot. The distance was close to four thousand meters and the target was slightly higher than our position. The captain had to estimate how much his two-hundred-pound projectile would fall while being fired slightly above the horizontal at four thousand meters. Not everyone on the hill knew the shot was coming, but we had a small crowd watching. It startled some Marines on the hill when the hog fired.

The two NVA on the ridge snapped their heads right to us. The sound of the 8-inch charge-three round being fired directly at them from even four thousand meters must have been terrific. At the same instant we had detonation, but the big bullet was high and hit fifty meters above the cave. Both NVA bolted back into the cave.

Back on the hill there was some disappointment from the gathering gallery, but the 8-inch gun captain was undeterred. He watched the explosion, made a quick calculation (one mil equals one meter at one thousand meters), ordered the muzzle down slightly, and the howitzer roared again. In just a few seconds the second round was on its way, and it detonated somewhere inside the mouth of the cave. I don't know where the two NVA went, or if there were any more NVA in the cave, but through the ship's glass I clearly saw the round detonate well inside the mouth of the cave, and smoke and fire belched out. Maybe not a great shot, but it was a very good shot. Through the morning we kept turning the glass back to the cave in hopes of seeing something move. Nothing moved up there, but it smoked all morning.

Two of the platoon commanders for Mike Company

were Terry Williamson and Duncan Sleigh. Terry was a journalism major from Pennsylvania, and Duncan would tease him about writing the great American war novel. Terry said that if he did, he would write it like Hemingway might, with the least number of words. According to Terry, "Hemingway said that some things must be experienced to be understood. 'I tell you I had a woman and she was good. If you have had a woman, you know what I mean. If you have not, no amount of words will ever explain.' That is the way combat is," Terry said. "If you have been there you understand; if you have not, no amount of explanation will work."

Duncan was from a Boston family and a graduate of Holy Cross. Terry teased Duncan about building a war record while he was young in order to be president sometime down the line. Duncan seemed embarrassed by the thought, but he never directly denied it. They were both good platoon commanders. They had both been in-country about four months. I respected the job they were doing and really admired them for doing it, but I was learning to like my job, and I would not have changed places with either of them.

3d Platoon was commanded by Lt. John Valentine. John had been in the bush for almost seven months. His replacement arrived while we were on Hill 52. It was another John, John Mason. The new lieutenant was from North Carolina. He had played college football, he was quiet, and he had a real Southern drawl.

If the company commander is the brains and authority of a rifle company, the gunnery sergeant is the energy and the enforcer. Gunny Gregory was no different. He was always "up," and he kept the company up and even. He had several favorite sayings, among them, "It is an honor to die for your country," "It's the amateurs in this world that give war a bad name," and my personal favorite, "What are you worried about? No one gets out of this world alive anyway."

It rained hard for several days. Human contact and communication were limited even though we were close together. It rained so hard that nothing happened and we were all ready for a break when, between rainstorms, word came out that it was the gunny's birthday. Private Timmons, the company runner, opened a C-ration pound cake and melted a chocolate bar over it, and someone else came up with a small candle.

A dozen or more Marines gathered close by as the gunny blew out the candle. "Speech" became a short chant and, as if he needed any prompting, the gunny spoke. "My wish just now as I blew out this candle is that each and every Marine here today feel as blessed as I do. I joined the Marine Corps the day after I turned eighteen." The Marine in front of me turned and said, "I can't fucking believe it; we are up to our butts in mud here and the gunny is giving a reenlistment speech."

I don't remember exactly what he said, but with the skipper smiling proudly on, and with some laughter as recognition dawned on the gathering grunts, Gunny Gregory gave a hell-raising reenlistment speech that would have made the commandant of the Marine Corps stand up and salute. There was no chance that anyone there that day would have signed up anyway, but before anyone could attempt to, the rain began to pour down again and flushed all of us back to cover.

Every war has prisoners of war. I was surprised after the war to find that so many Americans were POWs. It just didn't hit me that we were losing hundreds and hundreds of pilots. In the ground war that we fought, neither side took many prisoners. It was a war fought by small units, so perhaps it was too difficult for them to deal with prisoners. But we had to bribe Marines to bring back prisoners alive, and I don't ever remember the NVA or VC (Viet Cong) taking Marines alive.

Prisoners did give valuable information, I am sure, but most wars are fought bitterly on the ground, and Vietnam was no different. Late one afternoon we detained an old man for interrogation and had to keep him overnight. The gunny went to great lengths to ensure his safety. It seems that during that earlier stay on Hill 52, a VC had been captured and held overnight. During the night a Marine got up to take a leak and stumbled over the VC in the dark. Apparently several other Marines also had the same accident that night, because when the sun came up the next morning the prisoner had been "stumbled over to death."

Midafternoon one day, a lookout called out and fired his rifle toward Charlie Ridge. We quickly spotted a Vietnamese male in black pajamas about fifteen hundred meters out and walking away from us toward the ridge. He was much too far for rifles, so we called up 81mm mortars. There was a mechanical "mule" with a .50-caliber machine gun mounted on it that the "snuffies" (junior enlisted, private through sergeant, E1 through E4) called "rat patrol" after an old TV series. It pulled up and fired, and the target began to run. Next, a 106mm recoilless rifle pulled up and cranked off a couple of rounds, and then a tank roared up. As everyone scrambled clear, the tank fired several flechette rounds and then high explosives (HE), but the target continued to run. We were adjusting mortars on a moving target to no effect and trying to get a helicopter or aerial observer (AO) on the radio. By now there were more than a half dozen of the taxpayers' larger weapons all firing at high rates. The noise was terrific. The target kept running and running with dirt kicking up and dust flying all around him. He had covered almost a thousand meters at a dead run, with all kinds of projectiles flying past, when he suddenly pitched forward over a paddy dike and disappeared.

All the weapons stopped firing at once, and in the first moment of silence, Gunny Gregory cried out with great derision, "He must have had a heart attack!"

We had a patrol that by now was hunkered down about six hundred meters east; it took them fifteen or twenty minutes at a pace something short of double time to reach the spot. It was hot. We called them on the radio and told them where to look. They poked around for a moment and called us back.

"Mike 3, this is Mike 3-1. We found him, he's hit, he's not going to make it. I'm going to burn him. Over."

"This is Mike 3," the platoon commander, Lieutenant Valentine, called back. "If he is alive, bring him back to the hill. Over."

"Three, this is 3-1," the patrol leader radioed. "He's hit too bad. He'll die before we can get him there. I'm going to burn him."

"3-1, this is Mike 6." Now the skipper was involved. "We need him for S-2 [intelligence]. Don't burn him. I want you to bring him back here. Over."

"Six, this is 3-1." The squad leader was having none of it. "It's too hot. I'm not carrying a gook all the way back to the hill from here. Tell S-2 to come out here and get him if they want him. I'm going to burn him."

But the skipper was quick. "This is Mike 6. I'll give three days in-country R&R to the Marine who brings that VC back here alive." There was a long pause.

From three thousand meters we watched an animated discussion through the glass. After several moments of wrangling and a lot of gesturing, the patrol called us back.

"This is 3-1. Tiny says he will bring the gook back." Tiny was, of course, a mountain of a man who carried the VC, cradled in his arms like a baby, most of the three thousand meters back to the hill. Our enemy soldier turned out to be a kid about fourteen years old who had been hit in the ankle by a .50-caliber round. When Tiny trudged up to the company command post (CP), the kid's eyes were as big as saucers. His training had told him that if we caught him like this, we would eat him. But he looked a little bony and not much worth eating, so we called out a medevac from Da Nang and sent him to the "big lights" for treatment and internment.

Only a day or two later I was standing near the ship's glass when the earth began to shake, hard. Everyone seemed to freeze and go tense. The skipper stood up and said, "Arc Light," the term used for a B-52 carpet bombing. Next you could hear the low rumbling. The danger/close distance for Arc Lights was two thousand meters. But because we could not see anything at all, it must have been on the far side of Charlie Ridge, five or six thousand meters away. Nothing apparent was happening. We just stood there with the earth shaking for at least a full minute.

The amount of ordnance Uncle can put on a target is awesome. In any fight we ultimately had superior fire-power. It was referred to as the Three-F Principle: Find 'em, Fix 'em, and Fuck 'em. The war lasted almost ten years. We shot and shot; we killed thousands and thousands of them and still they came. I thought their determination was awesome.

Our efforts in support of Maui Peak lasted about three weeks, and then Mike Company was ordered back to Hill 55. As dirty and rough as life was on Hill 55, it felt like moving back to civilization. On Hill 52, we had eaten C rations and shaved in our helmets. But on Hill 55 we had ice, hot food, and hot water. I realized how I had taken for granted a wood floor and a roof.

The daily routine for an infantry company in the line can be backbreaking. Anytime they weren't on patrol or otherwise occupied, the troops filled countless thousands of sandbags. The Marine Corps, I think correctly, believes that the best way to keep young people out of trouble is to keep them busy and tired. To that end there was never an end to the activities the staff and officers came up with to keep the troops busy.

Captain Van Riper operated, most of the time, on a rather collegial basis. He often called the junior officers by their first names and he proved to be as much teacher as company commander. He might critique my activities by saying, "You may get better results by trying this." But he was quick and sharp with any officer who did not have control of his troops, or got behind the curve, or wasn't paying attention. Van Riper was also "plugged in." He had the latest and the best scoop.

There was always a poker game going on down under

the bridge. Many Marines in the company played in the game, but most of them lost money. One guy seemed to own the game. He took in whatever money was there. No one ever accused him of cheating, either. I don't think he had to.

We had been back on Hill 55 only a day or two when there came a rush to vote. Back in the World, Richard Nixon and Hubert Humphrey were in the home stretch of the presidential election. It seemed apparent that Nixon would win; he had campaigned on his secret plan to end the fighting and bring the troops home. I realized that in all the training and moving, I had never registered to vote. In 1968 you had to be twenty-one to vote. I was twenty-four, but the average age of the Marines in 3/7 was nineteen or twenty. That is directly the reason America lowered the voting age. It was also the last time I missed voting.

Rumor had it that as soon as the election was over, a lame-duck Lyndon Johnson would announce withdrawals. One way or another, this war would be over quickly. We might even be home for Christmas. I was really feeling torn. I would have been glad to go home, but in the month I had been in Vietnam, no one had really even shot at me, and I did want to be in a firefight.

November 4, 1630 hours or so. We had been back on Hill 55 for three or four days. It was too early to eat and too hot to sit where we had been, so Duncan Sleigh and I headed toward the staff club in search of ice and alcohol. We had been sitting there for ten minutes when we heard shooting off toward the southeast side of the hill.

You did not have to be in-country very long to learn a lot by just *listening* to a firefight. First of all, from the location of the fire, it had to be one of Duncan's patrols involved; second, there was a lot of fire going both ways; and third, a heavy automatic weapon was involved that was not ours.

Duncan and I bolted out of the staff club and almost ran into the skipper and two others who were hustling back from the mess hall. We covered the forty meters to Mike's CP in a pounding group so that the radioman had to tell his story only once.

It was Mike 2-2 (2d Squad, 2d Platoon) in trouble. They were on their way back from patrol, scheduled to arrive at 1600. At a turn in the trail they had found a bloody bandage and some blood spots. They followed and found more blood and drag marks. At that point they called in their find and informed Mike of their situation. They were at the edge of a large field about a hundred meters square that was an old burial ground. It contained two dozen or more mounds about four feet in diameter and height. They discussed the possibility of it being an ambush, but decided they could leapfrog from mound to mound, follow the blood trail, and reach the other side.

The point man was halfway across when he was shot once in the stomach. There was a lot of firing from both sides. When the second Marine moved forward to retrieve his buddy, he was killed. Mike 2-2 was a five-man patrol. With one dead and one down, the three remaining Marines found themselves pinned down behind three separate mounds and taking fire from two sides. We worked up a grid and got the 81mm mortars going. 2d Platoon's two other squads were already back from patrols and had been formed up as a reaction unit. Duncan took them at the double to reinforce 2-2. The skipper would round up 3d Platoon with John Mason and follow immediately.

At the river, next to the bridge, we had a watchtower about sixty feet high. We had placed our ship's glass on top. From there we could see the opening and the tree lines, if not the fight itself. I was sent there to direct covering fire and to coordinate fire. Van Riper took my scout-observer with him. India Battery could not shoot because the patrol was short on the gun-target line, which meant I would have to shoot the 155s and 8-inches from Da Nang, ten miles to our north.

As soon as Duncan arrived at the tree line with the rest of 2d Platoon, they moved out toward the trapped patrol. They took heavy fire and were quickly pinned down. A short time later the skipper arrived with 3d Platoon. They formed up and attacked the closest tree line, took heavy fire, suffered several casualties, and were quickly pinned down. Just as it grew dark, 1st Platoon formed up on the hill and moved out quickly to relieve the rest of Mike Company.

At night, war takes on a different feel. Sounds may seem sharper, as do smells, but in the dark the senses can become unreliable. Distance is tough to gauge, for example. Sounds may carry well at night, but sounds also move in the night air. Sounds can bounce around at night. At times in Vietnam, the fighting was only at night.

Mike Company was taking fire from ten to twelve rifles, a light automatic weapon, and a heavy 12.7mm automatic weapon. We had one dead and five or six wounded. The fight lasted until 0300 hours. Several Marines tried to reach the point man that night. Two, including my scout-observer, were wounded. The point man bled to death before anyone could get to him. He died there in the dark, crying for his mother. When Mike straggled back to the hill the next morning, we had two dead and six or eight wounded. And Mike Company was pissed.

We believed there was an NVA platoon reinforced with automatic weapons dug into an area along a small stream. The stream was the dividing line between 3/7 and the ROK's (Republic of Korea forces) TAOR. To avoid shooting at each other, the two units did not normally patrol up to the stream. We believed the enemy had moved into the vacuum. The old-timers referred to the area as Dodge City. We would take on replacements and reinforcements, and then Mike Company would go back into that little bend in the river, next to the graveyard, and rid it of enemy presence.

2

Lock and Load

I'm not scared of dying
and I don't really care
if it's peace you find in dying,
well then, let the time be near

If it's peace you find in dying,
and if dying time is here,
just bundle up my coffin,
'cause it's
cold way down there,
I hear that it's
cold way down there. . . .

And when I die, and when I'm gone
there'll be one child born
in this world
to carry on, to carry on

My troubles are many
they're deep as a well
I can swear there ain't no Heaven
but I pray there ain't no hell
Swear there ain't no Heaven
and I'll pray there ain't no hell
but I'll never know by livin'.
only my dyin' will tell. . . .
—BLOOD, SWEAT AND TEARS, "And When I Die"

It all begins with a five-paragraph attack order. Properly written, a five-paragraph order gives each soldier in the unit a precise knowledge of the necessities: objective, mission, and assignment. The company commander issues his order to the platoon commanders; they issue their orders to the squads in their platoon. If you do not have time to rehearse, writing a good order is even more important. Each of the five paragraphs has a specific purpose, from where and when to assemble beforehand to the kinds of attachments and support, to how and where we are attacking, and all the way through consolidation of the objective.

Mike Company swelled in numbers and plotted its revenge. We went from 130 Marines to more than 180. We added an FO for mortars, two more corpsmen to give us five, a FAC, and thirty or more riflemen to give us more punch. That afternoon, on November 5, the skipper gave us the order.

Mike would push off at 0600 the next morning. Our objective was the bow in the stream where we believed an enemy weapons platoon was dug in with two automatic weapons. We would cross the bridge in a column of twos and head south-southeast a thousand meters toward the objective. When we were five hundred meters out, the company would form into a "V" with 1st and 3d Platoons up and 2d Platoon, Duncan Sleigh's, back in reserve. The reserve platoon often exploits success, and Mike Company wanted some payback.

1st Platoon, on the left flank, would put one squad, the anchor squad, across the stream to the north side in case we needed to cross after contact began. Our mission was to close with and kill the enemy. We would consolidate in the tree line on the west side of the stream and make contact with the Korean troops, who were not attacking anyone—so as not to get in our way, I suppose.

We spent the rest of the day packing gear, making

maps, and preparing. It seemed that almost everyone saved cleaning weapons and writing letters for last. I had come to the war to fight communism, and now I would get my chance. We all knew the enemy would be ready for us, and everyone in Mike Company knew that by this time tomorrow, some of us in the company would be dead. It was a strange feeling, and I can tell you I was beginning to have some second thoughts.

At about 1800 hours a crowd gathered at the staff club. The battalion commander, Lt. Col. F. X. Quinn, and his staff, along with Kilo Company's CO and several officers and senior NCOs whom I did not recognize, would monitor the battle from Mike's CP on Hill 55 and be available to provide reinforcements and support. We drank a little, talked a lot, and even laughed a good deal. They talked of other Marines and told stories of other fights, and there was an atmosphere of cheer and quiet bravado—even though everyone did seem to be watching what they said. First call would be at 0400, so by 2100 the place began to clear out.

At 0100 the first of my prep fires began to fall. Each infantry battalion has a fire support coordinator (FSC). As the name suggests, his responsibility is to coordinate mortars, artillery, naval gunfire, and close air support for his particular battalion. Anything that goes *bang,* he should know first. For a preplanned assault like this, he and I had worked out a prep fire that started slowly, like H&I (harassment and interdiction) fire, and would grow to a "rolling thunder" by 0800.

At 0400 that morning the watch began waking people. By 0600 Mike Company had eaten, drawn ammunition, crossed the bridge, and headed out in a column of twos toward the objective.

We taped together dog tags, and all gear was taped or tied down. Every man carried a 60mm mortar round strapped to his pack. Upon contact, all the available rounds would be collected and shuttled to the mortars. Even with all that, it was surprisingly quiet. As I stepped off the bridge and into the brush, the loudest sound was the grass against my legs and an occasional *crunch* under my boot.

The silence was broken as the 155mm and 8-inch cannons at Da Nang sailed the opening rounds over our left shoulders. The rounds whistled high over our left flank and fell with a *krump* somewhere ahead, out of sight in the darkness. During the next two hours they would fire three hundred rounds into an area about four hundred meters square. Mike Company was being announced.

It quickly became light, and after twenty or thirty minutes the pace slowed as 1st and 3d Platoons fanned out. When the company reached the westward bow of the stream, Mike 1-1, a squad of ten Marines, crossed over to the east side of the stream and became our anchor squad.

As we moved close enough to see the objective, it became clear to me that most of the prep fire was missing the target. I called the FSC and told him the remaining rounds had to be moved 150 meters east.

I quickly discovered that you cannot just "check fire" during a planned prep fire. It took fifteen minutes or more for word to get back to 11th Marines in Da Nang and have a decision made to stop the firing and replot the targets. When the firing started again, only thirty or forty rounds may have been left. A few hit the target area, but many did not. Now I was basically out of bullets until we had contact or a live target. The company shrugged it off. It was business as usual.

As the stream turned from south back to the east the pace slowed again, and 3d Platoon wheeled around to face eastward—slowly now, probing for an enemy who must be there somewhere. It was after 0830.

The company crosses a semi-open area of high brush and heads toward another tree line. The growth is thick enough that I can see only ten or fifteen other Marines at any one time. Emerging from the tree line, fire teams from 1st and 3d move out into a large open field filled with burial mounds.

Courage: The state or quality of mind or spirit that enables one to face danger with self-possession, confidence, and resolution.
Devotion: Ardent attachment or affection, as to a person or cause; faithfulness, loyalty.

Even when you know the enemy is there, if he is well hidden and still, you will never see him in time. The point man on the anchor squad is twenty-five feet in front of the enemy's guns when he is shot once in the stomach and drops to the ground. Immediately there is a burst of enemy fire from the trees on our side of the stream. Advancing across wide-open ground, the first fire teams are only meters from the tree line when it bursts into fire. Marines in the two platoons return fire and move quickly, whether to attack the fire or take cover where no cover seems available. Several Marines from 3d Platoon stand up and charge the tree line, but they are shot down from two sides.

The second man in the anchor squad moves forward to help the point man and is killed. The third man in the anchor squad moves forward to help the second and is killed. In the first four or five minutes of the fight, the ten-man anchor squad takes 100 percent casualties: four dead and six wounded. Our left flank anchor squad ceases to exist.

It is not much better for the rest of 1st and 3d. Trapped in the open, the Marines fire when they can, but are so close they have the best luck throwing hand grenades. In a matter of minutes they have thrown all their grenades. Word comes back by radio and we quickly gather our grenades and shuttle them forward.

By this time the 60mm mortars have set up. They make some noise but seem to have little effect. Company headquarters has just reached what will be called the first tree line, and we are pushing into the trees when the shooting begins. There is no firing directly at us. It starts on our left flank and moves on our right. A high volume of fire, at first in both directions, soon changes to only incoming. We can hear the fight so near but can see nothing. Several of us start through the trees when Captain Van Riper yells at us, "If you look through those trees, you're dead. Don't do it!" He turns back to his handset and we momentarily freeze.

The enemy shoots the point man and then leaves him alive on the assumption we will not shoot artillery with a live Marine so close. They are right, of course. I scratch out a grid for the captain, but he quickly tells me no. Minutes pass and the volume of fire slows and becomes sporadic. Anyone in the graveyard who moves is shot, so no one moves. From behind the tree line we can stay down and move around somewhat, so we begin preparing for casualties. Mike Company has six dead and about twenty wounded.

The wounded point man and two of the KIAs (killed in action) from the anchor squad are still on the other side of the stream. I move forward a few yards to the observer group. A long burst of automatic fire comes through the trees directly at us, but a little too high. We are crouching over, trying to see through the trees, when four Marines come crashing out of the foliage right in front of us. They are carrying the four corners of a poncho. Slumped inside is Terry Williamson's platoon sergeant. I had met him the day before as we prepared maps for everyone. His shirt is gone, and he has a small puncture just under his sternum that looks like it might have been caused by a number 2 pencil. His skin is ashen white and he is dead.

Terror: Intense, overpowering fear.

Suddenly it hits me. I feel as though a cold steel claw inside my stomach has made a fist around my intestines. The Marines plow right past us and on toward the company CP. Someone waves them on another twenty meters to the side of a burial mound. We turn to follow them, but I am so terrorized that my stomach has involuntarily knotted. I cannot stand erect. I have to put my hands on my knees and physically straighten myself in order to stand up straight.

It takes thirty minutes or more to drag and carry the dead and wounded back to the burial mound where the LZ (landing zone) is being set up. Shooting erupts both ways as soon as anyone moves. An emergency medevac is called, and word comes that Kilo Company has come running from Hill 55 and is now just two hundred meters behind us, awaiting instructions.

The skipper leaves me with the radios and the gunny with the casualties. He heads back to Kilo to plan a second attack. 2d Platoon is helping treat the wounded, and they set out security for the LZ. The medevac chopper checks in in less than ten minutes. It is one of the old CH-34s. The pilots like them because they have two thousand pounds of engine mounted under and in front of the pilot's seat. They are dependable, too, but they are old and slow. That may be why there are not many left.

We have a "hot" zone, so when the chopper sets down, we will load only the emergencies and the wounded who can get on quickly. The others will have to wait for another bird. From my location twenty meters away, I watch the air controller flip a yellow smoke grenade so the pilot can judge the wind. The chopper comes in low from the north. As soon as he clears the last of the trees, I hear an enemy machine gun start up. The chopper comes down fast and begins to settle just on the other side of the burial mound partly out of my vision. Simultaneously, Marines collect their wounded comrades for the dash to the chopper.

At that moment, two enemy RPGs (rocket-propelled grenades) drop in right on target. One hits in front of the chopper and blasts holes in the engine. I see the second one through the strobe of the rotor blades. As it impacts on this side of the burial mound, the entire blast is absorbed by a group of five or six Marines hunched over next to the mound. They are blasted back and away from the mound. The company's S-2 scout staggers out of the smoke in my direction. I am running toward them when he stops and says, "They need help," and pitches forward on his face. The chopper takes off trailing heavy black smoke. It barely makes it the thousand meters back to Hill 55 before it crashes.

When I reach the mound, no one is moving. Two Marines are lying on their backs against the mound. One's face is gone and I can't recognize him. The other is the company runner, Pfc. James Timmons. I drop down next to him and realize that a yellow smoke grenade has ignited in the pocket of his flak jacket. As I strip the jacket from him, I notice he has a large wound in his forehead, another in his face, one in his chest, his throat is gaping open, and his left hand is hanging by tendons. Yellow smoke engulfs us and I gag until I can strip his flak jacket off and throw it clear.

Timmons is gurgling in his throat, and his chest makes a rattling sound. Call it first-time combat, but I am hunched over him pressing a bandage to his neck when he dies. And as he dies, his spirit leaves his body and passes through my body. It's not a religious experience; it is a very corporeal sensation. I won't try to explain it, but I am so shocked that I bolt up straight. From next to me I hear Gunny Gregory's voice shouting, "Timmons! No, God! Not Timmons."

The gunny jumps past me and grabs the dead Marine up in his arms like a baby and cries, "Please, God, don't take this one. Let me keep this one, God, don't take this one." Other Marines have arrived to help those still alive, so I turn and walk back to the radios. My arms feel as though they are on fire from the chemicals in Timmons's smoke grenade. I check my arms repeatedly for flames over the next few minutes.

The skipper comes walking back toward me and says, "Lieutenant Sleigh is dead. He and Timmons were killed together, trying to save one of the wounded." It had been Duncan's body that I could not recognize earlier.

I was as well trained for first-time combat as any soldier has ever been. In school we had studied sucking chest wounds and compound fractures during ROTC classes. The Marine Corps certainly spares no effort to provide a graphic understanding of what it is like when the bullets are real. Yet my mind had overloaded in the first few minutes of the fight.

I respond to the news about Duncan by saying something stupid like, "My arms feel like they're on fire." The skipper turns and walks back toward the activity at the LZ, and I cannot tell if his expression is one of pity or disgust. I simply sit there for several minutes and listen to the radios.

Another chopper reports in to pick up more of the wounded. This time no smoke is thrown. We use air panels—red-and-yellow three-foot-square plastic cloths set out by infantry to indicate their position to aircraft—and everyone who has to go gets out.

Time passes. My radio operator comes back with word about others who are dead or wounded. Mike has nine dead and more than thirty wounded. We have lost all five corpsmen.

I begin to feel very angry with myself for being so terrified and useless while Marines are fighting and dying around me. I tell my radioman to stay put with the radios. I pick up my radio and walk halfway into the trees, then lie down flat and begin to crawl into the graveyard toward a burial mound twenty-five meters in front of me. I am only a few feet into the open when an automatic weapon picks me up and opens fire.

The first burst is a little high, but obviously meant for

me. The second burst is very close and I realize what a foolish idea this is. Just ahead of me is a slight swale in the ground. I claw my way to it and press my whole body flat into the shallow depression. The trajectory of the machine gun means the bullets are grazing about a foot above the ground. He cannot hit me, and I cannot move.

I recognize Terry Williamson's voice up ahead: "Hardwick! What the fuck are you doing out there?!" I can twist my head around to see him hunched down behind another mound about twenty meters ahead. I stretch my arms out ahead of me and start to crawl for my life. I immediately get several bursts. My head is turned sideways with my cheek on the ground as a small bush next to my head is clipped by bullets and falls softly across my face. Finally I reach Terry and relative safety.

I have a grid coordinate with me and am prepared to begin shooting, but at that time Terry thinks the point man may still be alive, so he nixes the idea quickly. He sits for a moment silently and looks at his hands.

"I can't believe I'm alive," he says. He turns them over slowly in front of his face. "Look at me. Not even a scratch. I cannot believe I'm alive." We talk about the fight for a moment and the radio crackles to life. "All stations this net, be advised, Richard Nixon has defeated Hubert Humphrey and will be the next President of the United States."

In the midst of the fight, an eerie cheer rises up from the graveyard. Terry and I are leaning with our backs to the mound. Our heads are up but we can't see anything at all, not a person or any equipment, nothing. Yet this thin cheer fills the air. Some clapping and some whistles start slowly in the trees on our far right flank and spread through the graveyard around us and back to the tree line where the company CP is. America has voted against the war. The cheer is for our collective thought that maybe now somebody will get us out of here and send us home. The enemy gunners must think we have gone crazy.

I realize that I cannot function from any location in the graveyard, so I climb back into my swale and squirm my way back to the tree line. Charlie shoots at me part of the way, but finally gives up. Terry Williamson follows shortly. Once back at the CP, Terry calls me over to some gear collected from the casualties. "You see these two packs?" He picks up two and sets them out in front of us. "I know these two Marines very well. They are what the Marine Corps is all about. They were best friends. Now they're dead. I didn't inspect their packs before we came here. I knew they would be perfect."

He bends down and opens the two packs. Inside each is the prescribed gear, by the book. Each item is wrapped in plastic and neatly tucked into place. "We are losing our best," he says. "Duncan, these two, all the rest. This is stupid, man. This is stupid." He carefully tucks the items back into each pack. Later, we heard that more than three hundred people attended Duncan Sleigh's funeral in Boston.

There were a lot of ways to be killed in Vietnam. You could be "zapped," "dinged," "burned," "popped," "smoked," and more. The one that always haunted me was "wasted."

The first shot that morning had been fired at 0900. By now it was 1030 or 1100. We didn't know it then, but the fight was over. We stayed dug in there for two more days. That first night, Terry Williamson and three men from his platoon swam the stream to retrieve the three remaining Marines. The point man died well before we could reach him. For the rest of the time, we alternately dropped bombs and shot artillery, but Charlie had left the field.

The next morning at 0700 a chopper landed to pick up the rest of our dead. Off the chopper came four civilians: three men, two of them carrying cameras (one still camera and one movie camera), and a woman. As they walked up to us, they were regaling each other with a story about how they had been in Saigon drinking martinis just twelve hours before "when word came that a Marine company was in trouble." They had ridden choppers and jeeps all night before reaching Da Nang about an hour earlier.

The woman was in a raucous mood. "With the bombing halt up north and the election about to happen, the whole war has been on hold. You guys are the only action in-country right now." Looking past the civilians, we watched as our last six dead were loaded onto the chopper. Her cheerful words tasted like ash in my mouth. The man and woman were reporters from CBS and NBC. One of the cameramen belonged to them. The other cameraman was a French freelancer. A month later, while chasing VC with another Marine unit, he would be killed by a sniper. The four stayed for a couple of hours. The CO passed the word that we could talk about family, the States, or anything else, but not the war. They watched us adjust an 8-inch on some bunkers, and then they were picked up by another chopper to begin their journey back to the martini party in Saigon. Saigon, of course, is now called Ho Chi Minh City.

The rest of the day we sat, watched, and waited, and waited some more. The word was that tomorrow morning, with Kilo Company alongside, we would attack the objective and take it. It finally grew dark. I had targets registered all around us, but nothing moved. The night was punctuated only by our H&I fire.

Sunrise. The word changes: We will not attack. We pulled out our heat tabs and made coffee. I was still trying to digest all that had happened. Mike Company had suffered ten dead and more than thirty wounded. To the best of our knowledge we had not caused even one enemy casualty. We had taken a real hit, but by this afternoon we would be back on Hill 55 for hot showers and real food.

Two Marines walked toward us. "Are you the FO?" It was a platoon commander from another battalion. His voice was steady and quiet, but he had a strange look on his face.

"What can I do for you?" I asked.

"You killed a good man last night," he said, "and I just wanted you to know."

"I'm sorry," I said casually. "What do you mean?" The strange look on his face was grief, and his quiet, steady voice had a deep, intense anger behind it. He spoke slowly; he wanted me to hear each word; he wanted me to know how he felt.

"One of your H&I fires last night killed my corpsman, and I wanted someone to know. He was a very good man."

I heard his words, but I could not believe their meaning. "Come on. I'll show you," he said, so I followed him back to his platoon. His men were located on a high bank of the stream about two hundred meters away.

The opposite side of the stream was eight or ten feet lower and flat. They had moved in yesterday afternoon to reinforce us. Three 81mm mortar rounds had fallen there just at dusk.

"We heard them when they were fired from the hill," the platoon commander said. "The first one hit about fifty meters on that side of the stream. The second one hit in the stream, and we all scrambled for cover. He stopped to grab his helmet, but he never got it on."

The lieutenant showed me a fighting hole that had a broad field of fire overlooking the stream. The hole, dug years ago by one side or the other, had been maintained over the years by both. Dark splotches of blood soaked the freshly scraped dirt.

"The round hit here," the platoon commander said, pointing to a small detonation point. "A piece about the size of a quarter caught him in the back of the head and knocked a chunk out of his skull. He was out before he hit the ground, and he never regained consciousness. I made them leave the blood alone until you saw it. I was going to give you the piece of his skull, but someone sent it back with him this morning."

I asked questions, they answered. They had moved in at about 1600, two hours after we had cleared H&I targets. I could see what had happened, but I could not believe it.

I walked back to my gear and sat down in the foxhole I had dug. This really could not be happening, could it? I pulled out my map, identified the high bank at the bend in the stream, and carefully plotted the eight-digit coordinate. Then I pulled out my logbook and found the list of H&I fires I had cleared for battalion yesterday. And bingo! There it was. Not the same grid exactly, but much closer than the five hundred meters allowed for H&I fire near "other friendly units."

I had the location of other units marked on my map but none right there. As I sat in the dirt looking first at the map and then at the log, I was overcome by a wave of despair. How could this have happened? Until that time I had refused to believe the unfolding story. But I was the artillery officer responsible, and I had cleared that target. Why didn't the battalion fire support coordinator catch this? Why didn't someone tell me that Marines were moving into that location? *Why didn't I ask?*

I sat in my foxhole for several minutes and stared at my hands and then at my boots. It was me, but it *couldn't* be me. How could this have happened? I was still trying to get a grip on the losses we had suffered in combat. This was not even combat.

I felt sick. In 1968, I had never heard the term "friendly fire." Now, another American was dead and nothing could ever change that fact. How could we have killed, how could *I* have killed, another American?

I never met that corpsman. I never knew his name. I never even saw his face. But I will take his memory with me to my judgment.

We were ordered back to Hill 55 at noon. Fire teams had probed for the enemy and found him gone. When the word came to pull out, Mike Company simply stood up and walked away. I walked along with a dozen other Marines across the open graveyard to the tree line we had never reached. A low dirt berm about twelve inches high was where the foliage began. I stepped up on the berm and turned around to see what the enemy had seen. As you might expect, the spot was well chosen.

Mostly open, easy shooting with interlocking bands of fire. No one could get across if you didn't want them to.

It was a long thousand meters back to the hill. Column of twos out to the road, then turn north. The column was very quiet.

I was still feeling sick, sick in my stomach and sick in my heart.

It had not been a big fight, not even for Vietnam. But this war thing had turned into a real nightmare. Mike Company had its collective tail between its legs. My personal problem was that I still had a full twelve months to go on my tour, and I can tell you that I was scared. Deep-down-in-my-bones scared. I knew that if this was the way we were fighting the war, then none of us would survive a full tour. There was no question of leaving or of changing my situation. I had volunteered. There was no honorable way out, so leaving did not enter my mind. On that walk back, I gave myself up to the war. I could not visualize surviving twelve months of this and rotating. After that day, survival in the war became not a day-to-day experience but a moment-to-moment event.

My head was hanging when, back in the rear, somebody—Gunny Gregory—began to whistle the Marine Hymn. It sounded real corny at the time, and it still sounds corny as I write it today, but it worked like a charm. By the time he got a few bars into it, two, then three Marines picked it up. By the time he had finished and started through the second time he had the whole company whistling with him. At the finish he yelled, "Stand up straight, Mike Company! Be proud to be a Marine!"

I cannot speak for anyone else, but it probably saved

me. By the time we passed through the wire and were back on Hill 55, we were a Marine rifle company again. Fuck this waiting around, let's go pick a fight.

I learned five lessons from that first fight. One, unobserved fire seldom hits the target. Two, don't ever throw smoke in a hot LZ; use air panels. The pilots hate it and may whine about it, but don't use smoke. Three, I don't know why we did not have an AO for the first two hours of the fight, but in Vietnam there was an axiom: At the first sign of trouble, start calling up the most support you can find. Get artillery, get air, get the Pentagon if you can, but get help. Fourth, I did not need to carry a rifle. I had to cope with a map, compass, binoculars, and the radio. If the fighting ever gets to the point that I need a rifle, plenty of them will be lying around. Fifth, and most important: Before you shoot, check again.

The next few days on the hill were slow. The first day there were no patrols. I talked to the skipper and the battalion fire support coordinator about the corpsman who was killed by our mortars. The answer seemed to be, "That's a terrible thing to have happen, but this is Vietnam. It happens. Be careful." Friendly-fire casualties were not normally reported as such because the family then got nothing, not even a Purple Heart. All they can tell the family is, "You gave your child to the government and the government has accidentally killed him." So, most were reported as KIA.

The second day, Captain Van Riper sent 1st Platoon back to the bend of the stream. A brand-new second lieutenant had arrived to take over 1st Platoon, as Terry Williamson was being shipped to division HQ. The new guy was green. His name was Lee Neely, and he had been in-country about thirty-six hours. He looked soft and pasty and nervous as the skipper called us together before the patrol. Captain Van Riper wanted me to go along to provide supporting fire if we found something. I was to also provide Lieutenant Neely with counsel and perspective his first time out. Now that I had been under fire, the skipper seemed to trust me to help the new officers as each took over command for the first time.

The platoon moved across the bridge and covered the distance to the stream in a short time. We did not see anything until we reached the large field leading to the first tree line. Suddenly we started finding booby traps. As we moved across the field we found about fourteen small traps. Then we stopped. Some of the traps were in plain sight; it seemed as if Charlie was just trying to discourage us. We called the company and reported. I called for artillery fire on the tree line ahead of us, but without a live target we could get no clearances. Sergeant Bruneau, the platoon sergeant, and I looked at each other and decided we had seen all we wanted to see that day. We went back to the hill, where there was nothing but routine for two more days.

On the morning of the fourth or fifth day we awoke to the sound of helicopters. One landed at our LZ on Hill 55 and several flew low over the hill. I went to the door of our hooch with several other Marines and looked outside. In every direction the sky was full of helicopters. There must have been two hundred or more.

From behind us came the skipper's voice. "Operation Meade River," he said. "The largest combat airlift in Marine Corps history to date. They're lifting eight infantry battalions into the air at one time. The Marine

Corps doesn't even own enough helicopters to do the job. More than half of what you see is army choppers carrying Marines." We looked back at the sky and someone asked, "Where are they going?"

"Dodge City," came the answer. "They're going to clean it out once and for all. But we have our own business to attend to. We're moving." As we looked back at the sky, I thought about the fresh Marines coming straight in from a troopship who would very soon walk into that graveyard.

Operation Meade River lasted two weeks and the fighting was hard and close. Marines fought all day to gain a few yards and dropped lots of bombs and artillery rounds, but in the end the grunts had to root out the enemy by hand. Marines blew bunkers, then blew more bunkers. They dug out and destroyed a tremendous amount of supplies and equipment. On the last day, faced with advancing APCs (armored personnel carriers), many enemy soldiers broke. They threw down their weapons and ran. The APCs and infantry killed two hundred of them in one action.

We heard that more than one thousand enemy soldiers were killed in the operation and that the Marine Corps suffered eight hundred casualties (dead and wounded). We were also told that when the Marines finally left, the last chopper out took automatic fire from the ground.

The largest combat airlift in Marine Corps history. To think that it all began with a bloody bandage on the trail. I have always thought the experience was a powerful metaphor for the whole American involvement in Vietnam.

• • •

Unit rotation was common in Vietnam. Someone in the chain of command must have felt that moving a unit to a new location after it got its butt kicked was, well, refreshing. In any event, Mike Company moved from Hill 55, next to Dodge City, to Hill 10 in the "rocket belt." This belt was a one-hundred-meter-wide swath cut in a twelve-mile-distant arc around the air base in Da Nang. The maximum range for a 122mm rocket was something less than twelve miles.

Bulldozers had scraped off all vegetation inside the belt, and double concertina and barbed wire were stretched the whole length on both sides. Strong points— company strength or more—were located every thousand meters, with a watchtower every five hundred meters. A secret pneumatic tube of some kind ran the length of the belt underground and beeped on an audio monitor when it "felt" changes in pressure on the ground. We were told it would respond to footsteps, even small animals. That belt, along with constant patrolling, was to keep the enemy 122s from getting within range of Da Nang. Mike Company usually rotated platoons in and out, with two platoons out patrolling and one inside the lines on the hill. Sometimes the system even worked.

Hill 10 was battalion headquarters for 3/7 and the home of Golf Battery, 3/11. Golf would now be shooting for Mike Company, and while India Battery had to shoot charge-six or charge-seven most of the time, Golf was closer to many of its targets and shot mostly charge-two and charge-three. (Cannons add or drop charges with changing distance. 105s had a max charge of seven. Large cannons use a max charge of three.) As a result, its tubes were in much better shape, and so were its crews. Still, you could hardly be safe enough. The first round was always white phosphorus (WP or Willie Pete) instead of HE. Instead of shrapnel, the troops in the bush got a large plume of white smoke as a clear warning that more rounds would be coming.

Sacrifice: The forfeiture of something highly valued—an idea, object, or friendship—for the sake of someone or something considered to have a greater value or claim.

We soon discovered that war around the rocket belt was our very worst nightmare. We saw very few NVA. The war was fought against VC, and that meant mines and booby traps. Charlie often used our own ordnance against us. He dug up bombs and shells, and "acquired" explosives where he could. The resulting wounds were terrible. During the sixty days from November 15, 1968, through January 15, 1969, Mike Company would lose fifty-seven legs to mines. Everyone in Mike Company knew we were losing "a leg a day."

Later, the company clerk was careful to explain that we had not had fifty-seven mine incidents. We had had "only" about forty mine incidents, but some of them blew off both legs. On the other hand, he explained, the mines had caused other wounds (to hands, arms, eyes) that he did not even count, as though to assure us that we were really paying our fair share of dues.

It did not take much practice to read the signs and be able to tell on what the victim had stepped. A small box mine would blow double-ought shot straight up and in all directions. A 60mm mortar round would blow off one foot. An 81mm mortar round would blow off one leg at the knee and often get fingers, a hand, or sometimes an elbow. A 105mm howitzer round would blow off one leg at the hip, the other at the knee, and usually take an arm. A 155mm round would blow off both legs at the waist and kill any other Marines within twenty meters or so. After the second week, whenever the mede-vac pilots heard the call sign "Mike," we did not even have to give them coordinates; they knew where to go.

The mines were buried anywhere the dirt had been disturbed. They were especially bad in and around gardens or planted areas, and where trails intersected. One thing the manuals stress is not to have infantrymen "channelize," which means get too close together or walk in single file. Keeping the troops spread out in order to avoid casualties is a cardinal rule in small-unit tactics.

At first Mike Company resisted channelizing. But soon the toll from mines became so bad that Captain Van Ripper did what all good commanders do: He adapted to reality. After two weeks and perhaps fifteen or twenty mine incidents, he issued orders for all per-sonnel to stay on dikes and trails. The idea was to *not* step anyplace where someone else had not already stepped. The problem is that nothing works that way in practice, so the incidents slowed somewhat, but they continued with terrible frequency.

Whether you stepped on a mine or not was truly luck of the draw. As the whole company spread out across a large field, two squads split off to the right of a tree line. The skipper called me to move them back to our side. I walked through the trees and called to the troops, then walked back through the trees. The first Marine through was the platoon sergeant, who stepped through just be-hind me. Right behind him was a corpsman, who hit a box mine. It was almost always the same; first the boom and then the scream.

Sometimes they were planted in clusters. A Marine stepped on a mine that blew off his foot. The closest corpsman was a big guy with a fuzzy burr haircut. I am sure his mother always smiled when he walked through the back door. He was squatting by the injured Marine, and as he reached back for his bag he tripped another mine. It blew off both his legs at the hips and blew away his scrotum. He was still alive when we put him on the chopper, but that was the last I ever heard of him.

By the time a child is six or seven years of age, he has the manual dexterity to deal with explosives. The VC trained them early and used them effectively. One morning we had the company strung in a long single column on a dike. Several merging trails led to the village to our east. Our objective was farther south, so we never turned. We heard an explosion to our rear. Upon investigation we discovered two youngsters, each about seven years old. They had planted a mine for us at the first turn. When we passed by, they went back to dig it up. Their intention was to run ahead of us and bury it again, but it detonated, killing one and blowing several fingers off the hand of the other. We found their mothers in the village. We sent the wounded child along with his mother on a chopper to Da Nang. We paid cash compensation to the other mother for the loss of her child.

Surprisingly, our wounded left the field with the highest morale. To a man they seemed more concerned with those of us left behind than they were with their own wounds. Their attitude was, "I'm out of here, man, so I'm okay." It helped morale a great deal that we all knew the government would spare no expense to get you out once you were hurt.

The fighting near Hill 10 was virtually all at night. Different units would begin making contact about 2200, and there would be ambushes, chases, and chance encounters until 0300. There is an exciting, almost electric feeling you get when fighting at night. Nighttime offers both advantages and vulnerability. I loved it and I dreaded it.

A rifle platoon should have thirty-five riflemen, but our casualty rate was so high that platoons often had no more than fifteen or twenty. In order to cover our TAOR, night ambushes were often broken down into three-man "alley cats." In order to cover more ground, alley cats moved two or three times during the night.

Fighting the VC meant that kills were hard to come by. When we did get kills, it was often only one or two at a time. With Marines moving from place to place at night, it was inevitable that two patrols would cross paths and a firefight would ensue. It happened at least twice to Mike Company. At least once we had one Marine kill another. It happened to any rifle company that aggressively worked at night. During the day we had such a tremendous advantage in firepower that most daytime contact was little more than a chase.

One of the first replacements to arrive at Hill 10 was a new second lieutenant for 2d Platoon. The new platoon commander's name was Lou Piatt, as in "riot." Lou had graduated from seminary and decided not to stay in the church. He was a smart natural leader with charisma. Before he would leave Mike Company, he would win a Navy Cross and become almost a legend. Lou was daring at times, but seemed genuinely concerned for his platoon's safety.

Lieutenant Neely was having trouble getting his arms around the job. After two weeks, Captain Van Riper was ready to pull the plug and move him to another billet. The old-timers in 1st Platoon had gotten to know their lieutenant and liked him. The platoon trusted Lee Neely, and so the old-timers went to Captain Van Riper and had the skipper keep him. Lee Neely turned out to be a great success story.

On the other hand, Lou Piatt was in charge from the beginning. He seldom raised his voice, but he was prepared for the job and took over easily. Soon after, we got a first lieutenant, Tom Harrell from Louisiana. Tom had a bachelor's degree in chemistry and a master's in business. He was a scratch golfer and had talked about going on tour after Vietnam. Tom became the company executive officer (XO). By this time I was going with each platoon commander on his first couple of times out.

Mike Company quickly learned the perils of entering villages like Bo Ban 1 and Bo Ban 2, and Phuc Ninh 1 and Phuc Ninh 2. They were not so much villages as clusters of a dozen or so thatched huts, but they had mines everywhere. We had perhaps twenty little villages in our TAOR. In eight or ten of them, about half, we had serious mine problems. In other places we had serious sniper problems. In all of them, we swept around, day and night, looking for the enemy and/or supplies the enemy could use. If we decided a village had too much food, we dumped the excess. The decision was sometimes arbitrary.

Most Marines learned how to deal with Vietnamese

civilians in sometimes awkward ways. Most of the civilians spoke no, or very little, English. Most Marines only knew four words or phrases in Vietnamese: *dung lai* (stop), *la dai* (come here), *di di* (leave), and *di di mau* (get the fuck out of here).

During my time with Mike Company, I never saw Marines burn hooches or wantonly destroy, torture, or kill noncombatants. The policy was to win the hearts and minds of the people while at the same time waging a war of attrition on an indigenous guerrilla force. I can tell you from my experience that it is easier to explain that policy in a briefing room than it is to execute it in the countryside.

Vietnam provided a number of unique experiences. I participated in only a few night ambushes, and we never got anything but stiff muscles. Because I was the FO and carried only a service .45, I would be half useless in a firefight, anyway. My radio operator and my scout both carried rifles, but we preferred to let the grunts do the fighting. Our job was to call for supporting artillery fire, and we became very good at it. Even though I was an officer and often the highest rank around, I tried to stay out of the command structure. Ambiguity of command is not good, and no one wants to be second-guessed. I kept to my job of supplying supporting fires and did not issue orders or countermand the grunts. If a corporal or sergeant was the patrol leader, I would offer suggestions only if asked. The grunts knew where they were going and what they were doing better than I did, so I tried to be constructive and stay out of their way.

The skipper had me develop a method for shooting at night. He wanted to cover spaces our patrols had vacated, or cover spaces our patrols did not reach. Even had we been staffed at full strength, our TAOR was too big for us to effectively stop the enemy's movement at night. We were running at only 55 to 60 percent strength, yet even being spread so thinly, we had hopes of flushing the prey into one of our traps. I cannot tell you that the strategy ever worked, but it did mean that the patrols had to get up and move periodically during the night.

It is very difficult to keep up with your exact location at night. Fatigue becomes a problem. Even if you shoot an accurate azimuth, distance is tough to judge without seeing major landmarks. Terrain often makes movement in a straight line impossible. If a patrol moves twice at night and ends up three hundred meters out of place, and the first round we fire is even a hundred meters out, you could have a conflict. For that reason the first round was always WP.

It did not matter that Charlie also knew that a WP round would be followed by HE. Our purpose was to make him turn. For one reason or another, our efforts sometimes succeeded. Mike Company was aggressive, and in a very real sense the killing at night sustained us through the terrible losses we suffered during the day. We never hit a mine at night, and that made me, at least, feel stronger. Because their own troops and supplies moved at night, Charlie seemed to pick up his mines at dusk.

I don't know where morale might have gone, given our casualties during the day, had it not been for our success at night. The mines had a devastating effect on everyone. We were two or three weeks into the carnage when I was part of a bizarre conversation that gave our situation away. Lou Piatt, Lee Neely, and I were in our hooch. Lou was writing a letter to the family of a Marine who had just been killed by a large mine.

"I think I would turn in the lower part of one leg to Supply," said Lou, "if they would let me keep my knee."

"And, of course," we offered, "catch a plane home this afternoon."

"Of course," Lou replied.

The argument went something like this: In all honesty, you don't really need both feet, do you? As long as you can still touch the earth with one good limb, isn't that enough? After all, with today's prosthetics, if you could keep your knee, it's doubtful you would even have a limp. Think of the advantages. First, a clean surgical procedure. No shrapnel, dirt, debris, or ugly jagged mess. Second, and very important at the time, was certitude. The anxiety and insecurity of never knowing who would be next or what kind of wound it would be weighed heavily. This voluntary option was clean, neat, and certain. It had a strong emotional pull; like the mouse that wants no more cheese, just out of the trap.

John Mason and Tom Harrell came into the hooch. "Quick, guys, if you could turn in one leg today at Supply and go home, would you do it?"

The first question they asked was, "Can I keep my knee?" And the second question was, "Can I go home today?" We drew the line at the knees. There did not seem to be a clear second choice, such as both feet versus one foot and one knee.

John was feeling a little shaggy and Tom had a pair of clippers. The idea was to edge a little at the ears and the neck. I do not remember how it got started, but the next thing I knew the five of us were bald as cue balls. We looked like brand new "boots" with our heads shaved.

We felt more like condemned men awaiting an uncertain execution.

December 8, 1968. One year after commissioning, my officer class was promoted. I had heard that after one year we became first lieutenants, but I never thought it would be to the day. Captain Van Riper called me to the CP, and when I arrived he shook my hand and handed me a pair of silver bars. He then read the accompanying proclamation and shook my hand again. It was almost like being accepted. I am told that you are not really accepted until you get captain bars, but still it felt good.

Sometimes both sides did the same things for different reasons. We recovered our dead and wounded for esprit. A Marine knew that if he got wounded, then everyone and all of Uncle's resources would be used to get him out. No one was ever left behind. On the other hand, the enemy recovered his dead and wounded simply to keep us from getting an accurate count. Charlie was faced with having to move fast and light and still extract his fallen. They would often put a loop in a rope and throw it around the victim's feet. Then one or two VC could drag a dead comrade and still carry their loads. Or Charlie had another option, one that stopped me cold when I first heard about it.

Feel with your thumb and forefinger at your ankle, where your Achilles tendon attaches to your heel. Between the tendon and the ankle bone is a fleshy, empty space. The VC would lay the corpse on his back and hook his feet together with a suitable hay hook or meat hook. Or they would cut a slit with a knife and run a stick through to make a handle. With the corpse thus engaged, a man could pull with one hand and still have one hand free; or two men could grab the handle and evacuate the area smartly.

Occasionally we flushed Charlie out during daylight. There is hardly a more exciting way to spend a sunny afternoon than chasing men with guns. Something moves, or someone steps from concealment. There is a shout or a shot, and the chase is on. All we really saw of Charlie during daylight was his heels. They seemed to move three or four at a time. When we caught them, we killed them, but they were hard to catch. They always had at least one black pajama, a local VC, with them, someone who knew the hiding places and exits.

One afternoon five enemy soldiers were spotted headed south toward Kilo Company; they were in a hurry. Those of us close to the area saddled up and gave chase. A patrol from Kilo could see the river where the enemy would likely cross, and we shot in a blocking target to the west with Golf Battery. They passed through a village and turned slightly west across five hundred meters of open paddy to another village next to the river. With Kilo watching the river, we could trap them in the village.

My patrol arrived at a nearby tree line and worked its way south and west to a place where the trees came within two hundred meters of the village. Ten or fifteen members of Mike Company were already gathered there. We continued spreading out and forming units as more of us arrived. In about twenty minutes the skipper arrived. He brought with him several South Vietnamese from the National Police Field Force. A platoon of thirty had been assigned to 3/7 and, rather than split them up, they were all assigned to Mike Company. The captain had brought their platoon commander, the interpreter, and two others along with all their radios.

At that point we knew that five enemy soldiers armed with at least four rifles had entered the village and not been detected leaving. The interpreter had brought a battery-powered bullhorn. While the skipper had me crank up the artillery, a Vietnamese voice came squawking out of the small speaker. The voice told the villagers that we had not come to hurt them. We were pursuing our common enemy, the VC. They must leave the village at once or risk being killed in the action that was about to take place.

Nothing happened.

By this time I had sixty or seventy Marines short on Golf Battery's gun-target line. Kilo's units were a little south of west, which made India Battery my closest support. India fired a first round, Willie Pete. While the round was on its way, the speaker told the villagers again that it was dangerous to stay and that they must please move out of the village and into the paddy so no one would get hurt.

Nothing moved.

The WP round landed in the paddy right next to the village. From the skipper: "Give me a battery one" (all six guns firing one round each).

I called back to India, "Right five-zero, battery one."

India fired a battery one. Seconds later, five rounds crashed into the village, but the sixth 105 round landed way long. It cleared the five hundred meters of paddy the VC had vacated and landed somewhere near a village, in the trees there. I called India and told them we had one gun shooting long and to check their charges; one of the guns must have fired a charge-seven instead of a charge-six. Next we shot a battery two and all the rounds hit in or around the village.

By this time we had almost the entire company formed up in the trees two hundred meters from the village. The word came down: "Fix bayonets." If that doesn't make the hair stand up on your neck, you still don't understand what is about to transpire.

The speaker worked again. "Come out. We do not want to hurt you, but you must come out."

Nothing moved.

I shot India several times, and the speaker talked. I shot several more times, and the speaker talked again.

We had seen only five enemy and only four rifles. Still, the men of Mike Company were not eager to hang themselves out across two hundred meters of open paddy. We shot and squawked, shot and squawked. This went on for quite a while.

Nothing moves.

India Battery calls, "We have fired 227 rounds. Is something going on we should know about?" At that moment an AO checks in with a flight of F-4s: napalm and 250-pound bombs.

The speaker announces to the village, "We have been patient with you, now we have bombs. Come out so you will not be hurt." An F-4 lines up and drops a warning bomb short of the village, and Mike Company pushes out of the trees and into the paddy. Bayonets gleam in the sun. Heat rising from the paddy gives the tree line ahead of us a shimmering effect. Halfway across the open paddy, cone hats and black pajamas come flooding our way from the village. Lou Piatt is the first to reach the oncoming horde. He looks carefully at several, stooping and craning to see all he can. "Good shooting, arty! Two hundred twenty-seven rounds and we have no wounds. Not even a headache."

The villagers know we are shooting 105s, and that 105s cannot penetrate their bunkers. When the presence of bombs is confirmed, they vacate, safe and sound. Not so the livestock and exposed belongings. After 220-plus artillery rounds, the village itself is trashed. We sweep through, consolidate, and begin to search. At the same time the battalion S-2 tallies the destruction and opens negotiations with the villagers for cash compensation. 3d Battalion does not have enough cash on hand, and the S-2 will have to return tomorrow. The villagers will still be there. The most valuable possession the people own is a water buffalo. In Vietnam we paid more for killing a water buffalo than we paid for killing a child.

The search reveals nothing. Either the VC have split or they are hiding so well that we cannot find them. So Mike Company returns to the hill in time for dinner.

The next morning just after first light, there was a shout from the bridge. I was awake but not up when someone stuck his head through the hooch door and yelled, "Okay, artillery! You got some yesterday!"

I pulled on my trousers and boots and walked out of the hooch toward the road. Already across the bridge and almost up the road to us was a cart being pulled by a water buffalo. Four Vietnamese accompanied the cart, one at each corner. At least one was wounded. On the cart were two dead bodies and two badly wounded Vietnamese.

When India Battery had fired its first battery one yesterday, five rounds had hit the target area and one round was long by several hundred meters. These villagers were having a community meeting when the long round detonated next to the group. One was killed immediately. Because it was getting late, they had to stay in their bunkers until morning. Another died during the night. Before first light they began their journey to our aid station.

As they creaked up the hill, Marines briefly stopped shaving or talking to watch quietly for a moment before going back to their business. No one moved to help them. They had gotten this far because of us and without us; they knew the way to the aid station.

I stood beside the road for several minutes and looked at the destruction one long round had caused. I did not feel good, but I did not feel that bad. I was numb to their losses. After all, these were the same assholes who knew where every mine and booby trap was located and had never lifted a finger to help a Marine.

Hate: To loathe; detest; strong animosity.

I was learning how. All of that said, I would not have traded the whole exercise for even one slightly wounded Marine. I will say it again: Winning their hearts and minds while waging a war of attrition was a difficult policy to execute in the countryside.

Other afternoons were not so good. I was with two squads patrolling just southwest of the hill. We moved through a mostly deserted village, into a small opening, and across to the tree line. Ahead was 150 meters of paddy to the next tree line. You do it all day long, and it can become mind-numbing.

When the point man is barely twenty-five meters into

the open, a four-round burst of AK-47 fire comes from the far tree line. Three rounds are high; they clip through the trees. The first round, however, finds its target. The point man is down, yelling that he is hit in the hip.

M-16s open fire at the far tree line as two Marines race forward, grab the point man, and carry him back to us. A concrete table is close by; the wounded Marine is laid on the table.

An emergency medevac is called. They usually arrive in less than fifteen minutes. Our man is strong. He talks about going home and what he will tell his family about us. The wound is worse than anyone thought. The bullet entered through his left hip, but it glanced off bone and traveled diagonally up through his body, exiting high on his right side, beneath his armpit. The corpsman finds the exit wound and squints his eyes closed.

No one says anything. The wounded Marine is unaware. Six to eight minutes pass. Our man is growing quiet. "I'm going to be okay," he tells us. "I'm going to make it. I'm going home." But he is having trouble breathing now. It is ten minutes since the chopper was called. He is still and quiet. His eyes are open, but he does not speak. His breathing is labored, shallow. "Hold on, buddy," someone says.

Marines look away, trying not to stare. Twelve minutes have passed. The chopper checks in on the net. The crew is ready to get another Marine out of the war and back to the World, but our man is dead.

I cannot describe the grief and the anger and the frustration that can well up inside watching the life seep from a strong, vibrant comrade. Those are feelings that you don't easily forget.

● ● ●

Before Captain Van Riper became the CO, Mike Company had burned hooches and destroyed property in retaliation for sniper incidents. The skipper put a stop to it. But we did not control the South Vietnamese Rangers attached to us. On an all-day sweep with John Mason's platoon, we had the Rangers with us. After dodging sniper fire for much of an hour, we finally chased the shooter down to a small village. We encircled the village and moved in with the Rangers to question the villagers. I did not expect that they would give up the shooter, but we might get lucky. Once in the village, the Rangers took charge. They rounded up everyone, about ten people: old men, women, and children.

We had a German shepherd scout dog with us. The Vietnamese were terribly afraid of the shepherds. For that matter, so was I. The Rangers asked questions, but no one responded. They dragged out a youngster and asked for the dog. The boy was about nine or ten years old. They put the dog close to him and held the young boy by his neck and his shirt from behind. They asked a quiet question and when the boy did not respond, they nodded to the dog trainer. He gave the dog a command and the dog lunged at the kid, barking, snarling, slobbering, pawing right up in the kid's face. You could see fear in the youngster's eyes. His body was trembling, flinching, but he said nothing. The Ranger screamed a question at him and the shepherd lunged so hard he managed to get his teeth on the boy's arm. No blood was drawn, but I thought the youngster might collapse from fear. Still he said nothing. It was a very gutsy display.

Moments later a young Vietnamese woman about twenty years old appeared. Immediately the Rangers let go of the boy and grabbed her. I don't know where she had been hiding, but she was obviously giving herself up in order to protect the boy.

At least two Rangers were asking questions. She seemed to answer several questions, but not to anyone's satisfaction. They dragged her to a concrete table and slammed her down on her back. One Ranger put a rag over her face and another began to pour water from his canteen onto the rag. I had heard of this before but had never seen it done. It gives the impression of drowning without actually doing it.

From her frantic kicking and struggling she believed the worst. They removed the rag and asked questions. She coughed and spat, gasping for air, then she said something they did not like. They pushed her head back down and started to pour water again. By that time John Mason and I were looking at each other. Two Westerners with weak stomachs.

John pulled one of the Rangers back and stopped the proceedings. John was hesitant. This was, after all, their country, and we were invited guests. He was talking to the platoon commander, who was consoling him.

It was torturous, the soldier told John, but it would do no actual harm. The Ranger was telling John through the interpreter that she was the wife of a VC squad leader, and that she was the one who had sniped at us all afternoon. John was wavering as to what to do when one of the Rangers holding the girl grabbed her trousers and pulled them down to her ankles. With that, several Rangers began to unbuckle their belts and shove each other to get in line. That was enough for John, and he shouted right past the Ranger platoon commander, "Bullshit!"

In a deep Southern drawl, he said, "There will be no boom-boom here today!" Two Marines stepped up to the table, pushed the Rangers out of the way, and stood the girl on the ground next to the table.

The Rangers became angry and quite agitated with us. The interpreter shouted, "This is wrong! You cannot tell us what to do. We must report this to your superiors."

John was smiling now and said, "I don't care what you report. There will be no boom-boom here today."

For a moment it appeared we might have a standoff. But it was getting late and it was decided that we would head back to the hill. As we left, the villagers were all frozen in place. The girl stood there with her pajamas down at her ankles. Her long black hair was shining in the sun. Her eyes were large and staring straight ahead. It may have been fear on her face or simply hatred, but she was beautiful, almost regal.

The Rangers talked loudly to each other all the way back to the hill. Because none of us spoke Vietnamese, we never knew what they said. If we had, there might have been a fight. Nobody was happy that day.

I saw some great shots in Vietnam. One sunny afternoon we had a platoon pursuing an unknown number of enemy soldiers. They were running through trees somewhere ahead of us. Several of us broke out of the trees into a long, narrow paddy to see a lone VC beating a fast path two hundred meters ahead. He appeared to be running for a thatched hooch about three hundred meters from us.

Just ahead of us, a young Marine came walking out of the trees hurriedly snapping together a 3.5-inch rocket launcher. He stopped and loaded the only round he had, a WP round. He squared up into a firing position, facing the rapidly receding enemy soldier. He lined up his tube and raised it like a latter-day Robin Hood arching an arrow. He hesitated several seconds to see if the VC would head into the hooch or run past. As the black pajamas veered toward the hooch, the rocket was fired.

These things are best observed from safely behind and slightly out of the way, but you can see the slow antitank round all the way to the target. The VC went through the door of the hooch at the very instant the Willie Pete round went through the window. The old thatched hooch exploded in a great white fireball. The tree line to our right exploded into a loud cheer. "No shit! Did you see that?" Marines said as they turned to smile at each other. It was a terrific shot, the kind that can get you a reputation or even a nickname in a rifle company. No one was willing to walk the three hundred meters to the flaming hooch and back to check on the results. But the rocketeer got a confirmed kill and the company got a morale boost.

I was with Lou Piatt's platoon on one of his first patrols, and we were about fifteen hundred meters south of Hill 10. We had discovered some bunkers and tunnels that seemed to be used occasionally. There was no sense in leaving the enemy a dry place to sleep at night, so we decided to blow the whole bunch. We had brought a good deal of explosives to do just that job, but we continued to find more things to blow and shortly ran out of C4 (plastic explosive). A squad leader called to Lou and motioned him to a large tree. We had one more aboveground bunker to blow, and one or two blasting caps, but no C4. The squad leader pulled up some branches on the tree to expose a 155mm round. A common flinch went through us as we realized what we had.

It appeared to be just lying there, as though someone had rolled it under the tree for safekeeping. We'd already had bitter experiences with booby-trapped American artillery rounds, so I could not help but feel a little twitchy crouched over this ugly, cold projectile.

"I have a fuse and caps, Lieutenant," said the lance corporal in charge of the blasting, "but I'm not going to move it."

Lou looked at me and said, "It's one of yours; do you know what to do with it?"

I could see that the fuse had been unscrewed and removed. The white chalky explosive was plainly visible. There did not appear to be any other holes, wires, or attachments. "Sure," I said confidently, "I'll put it in the bunker and blow it. It weighs eighty pounds, and at one pound per meter, get your people eighty meters away, and down."

As Lou moved his platoon out and away, I got on my hands and knees and felt my way over to the projectile. I was leafing through the dusty pages of my mental notebook to a Saturday morning class in frozen Quantico. The instructor was going to great lengths to show us how stable and safe these explosives were. With the fuse gone, they would have to drill a hole in this thing somewhere in order to booby-trap it. The ground was hard and had not been disturbed. I felt under and around the shell, and it did seem to be just lying there. I picked up the round, carried it over to the bunker, and went inside.

The bunker was about five by eight feet and very much like other ones that had taken direct 105mm hits without a problem. I used my K-bar knife to dig a hole in the explosive inside the fuse opening and packed in the blasting cap with a thirty-second fuse. I knew the 155 round would probably destroy the bunker, but I had no idea how big a bang it would make.

"Fire in the hole!"

I caught up to Lou about eighty meters out and we half lay, half reclined against a ten-inch-high dike.

"Is this going to work?" he asked.

"Oh, yeah," I said expectantly. Two seconds later a gigantic explosion blew everything everywhere. Shrapnel, dirt, debris, and some kind of leafy stuff were blown well past the two of us. A large wall of dirt rolled partway toward us before settling.

As we got up and dusted ourselves off, Lou's eyes were a little larger than usual. "Did you know that would happen?"

I gave him a weak smile as my stomach did a flop.

"Let's go, Mike 2, we're out of here," he called.

Lesson six in Vietnam: A dirt bunker is designed to take a lick from the outside. When pressured from the inside, it comes apart like a paper bag. But all's well that ends well. Lou looked back again, and I gave him a stronger smile. We all made it home for dinner that night.

The "body count" was a strange tally, used and abused. But how else do you know if you're winning or losing in a war of attrition? So the body count became an important yardstick up and down the chain of command. At times you could not confirm a kill without showing an enemy weapon, documents, or a piece of clothing as evidence. At other times, some headquarters group might simply assign a body count to some action, knowing or believing that they had hit something while being unable to put anyone on the ground to investigate. All kinds of ways of counting went on between the two extremes. You can bet that every squad, every company, and every battalion knew its body count and its kill ratio. They might not talk about their kill ratio unless it was very good, but most units knew what it was. I never considered a kill ratio of less than ten-to-one to be a decent trade.

There are fifty-five thousand dead or missing Americans from the Vietnam War. North Vietnam had a population of seventeen million when the war began, and I can easily believe that we killed five hundred thousand of them. I have always maintained that we did not lose the war in Vietnam, but that we quit. Even so, with that kind of kill ratio and that kind of effort, the North should have given up. The Vietnamese scored the war differently. To Ho Chi Minh and the North, every day they could fight was one more day they did not lose. And in the end, their way of counting prevailed.

At night in most any command bunker, you worked under a red light. Red light does not impair your night vision like regular incandescent light does. About midnight in early December, several of us were in the Mike Company CP when we heard M-16s firing to our southwest. It was obvious to us that Kilo Company had sprung an ambush, so we switched the battalion radio over to Kilo Company's net. Everyone in Vietnam eavesdropped as much as possible.

"Kilo, this is Kilo 3-3. We have sprung an alley cat [ambush] and we have one confirmed and at least one, maybe two, wounded. Over." It was a whispering, excited voice on the radio.

"Roger 3-3. You have sprung an alley cat and have a confirmed. Wait one."

The next voice we heard was Kilo's CO: "This is Kilo 6. Good work, 3-3. Can you get the other two?"

"This is 3-3. I don't know." He was still speaking in a whisper. "They disappeared, but one was hit and I can't believe we missed either one. The three were right in front of us. Over."

"Are you at the body? Where is the body? Over."

"He's down, in the open, about thirty feet in front of me."

"Do you have his weapon? Did he have any documents?" The CO did not sound impressed.

"I haven't checked him, but he's dead. Over." A sound of exasperation was creeping into the young Marine's voice.

"You don't have a confirmed yet, 3-3. Bring me something, a piece of clothing, if you want a confirmed kill. Six out."

Someone in our bunker mutters, "You fucking lifer." Several seconds pass.

Someone else in our CP mutters, "Don't move, man! Wait for daylight. You're not rotating tonight: stay put."

Several more seconds pass, and the silence is broken by a burst from an AK-47. Shortly after, four shots are fired from an M-16. Half a minute passes in silence.

A different voice comes on the radio. "Kilo, this is Kilo 3-3. Cancel that confirmed. Instead we have one KIA. I hope you're happy, you son-of-a-bitch." The voice dripped with anger.

Our whole room sagged. He should have stayed still and just watched until daylight. Now he was dead. He did not have to move, but the CO should never have goaded him. I doubt that anyone in Mike Company would have walked into a kill zone in order to check a body.

Kilo 6 came back on the radio. He exchanged information with a third voice and told him he was sending the rest of their platoon to relieve them. Removing a dead Marine by helicopter was classified as a "routine" medevac—there was no rush—and we could not send a routine medevac out there at night. Still, no one wanted to leave him there all night.

In the middle of December, Captain Van Riper ordered all nonessential personnel to stay off daily patrols. That meant that several of us—observers, radiomen, the XO, even the gunny—would no longer be making patrols. A rifle company is a close-knit team, very interdependent and very proud. Everyone wants to carry his share; no one wants a free ride. That's the Marine Corps. Even though I was an attachment, being branded nonessential for any reason was something of a blow. As a consolation the skipper gave me command of the watchtower. I felt relieved.

The watchtower was located halfway between Hill 10 and the hill that was Kilo's CP. The terrain from the tower north to the far western edge of Hill 10 had needed no bulldozing. It was flat and open, and the enemy very seldom ran that part of the barrier. The terrain from the tower south to Kilo's CP had been scraped off, but the dirt and scrapings had been piled in several long rows that masked rifle and machine-gun fire between the tower and Kilo's CP. Perhaps 80 percent of the crossings in our TAOR came through right there.

Some nights the pneumatic tube made sounds all night on its audio monitor. Some nights it seemed to be dead. But several times a week we would get positive readings, and we quickly learned the difference. The tube was supposed to give us a reading on distance so that we could direct fire or move a blocking force. I could never confirm its accuracy. We set up claymore mines at different distances and cranked them off in response to readings we believed were positive. We fired the mortars and machine guns, but I could never tell if we hit anything. On some occasions after we shot, we would form a line between the two wire barriers and sweep out from the tower several hundred meters. Several times we had Golf Battery involved. On one occasion, after firing twenty or thirty rounds inside the barrier and on both sides, we found lots of blood and drag marks, but we never got a confirmed kill.

The primary job we had at the tower was to alert nearby units that Charlie was on the move. His purpose was to move troops or rockets, or both, closer to Da Nang. Lou Piatt's platoon once recovered sixteen 122mm rockets from a lake in which they had been hidden.

The closer we came to year's end, the more troops Charlie was moving. At times you had to wonder how he could move up to fifty or sixty troops through our TAOR and not run into us. At other times we could not seem to get out of the way.

3

Their Hearts and Minds

C'mon people now,
Smile on your brother
—THE YOUNGBLOODS, "Get Together"

December 25, 1968, Christmas Day, was pretty much like any other day. Just after noon my scout-observer and a half dozen other Marines singing carols made the rounds to several hooches. Yes, we were all homesick. But Mike Company was having improving luck at catching Charlie, and we felt we were learning how to fight an elusive enemy.

I spent every other night at the tower and the alternate nights at Mike's CP. In order to do the shooting that we had scheduled each night, I needed light and a flat place to work. At 2200 on Christmas night, the tower reported a large movement at the three-hundred-meter mark.

Lou Piatt's 2d Platoon was scattered in several different locations on the east side of the wire. To cover more ground, each of the three squads had broken into two units: a main ambush and an alley cat, usually three men, somewhere close by.

With the enemy on the move, we fired a preset illumination target at the three-hundred-meter mark. Almost immediately one of 2d Platoon's ambushes reported a group of twenty to thirty enemy troops passing out of the wire and heading east. The ambush took the group under fire, but from too far a distance to be effective. They did, however, turn the group north along the east side of the wire.

We had them in a box: the wire on the west side, Hill 10 on the north end, and Marines pursuing from the south. Now we had to block the east side with the rest of 2d Platoon. The ambush pursued to the north and east hoping to intercept the enemy when they inevitably turned back east. Along the way they joined up with Lou and another squad, and they all headed north and east.

Back in the CP we were all poring over our maps. I was moving illumination rounds and trying to get a platoon of guns from Golf Battery to fire HE into a fifty-meter-square zone east of the wire and two hundred meters south of the tower. A trail ran east from the barrier to a small village located four to five hundred meters east and midway between the barrier and the main north-south road. The best guess was that the enemy would have to use that trail or move closely parallel to it.

2d Platoon had two squads together headed north toward the village. The other squad was east and just to the north of the village. Its three-man alley cat had split off to a finger of a tree line that was two or three hundred meters north of the village and projected out to the west. Lou wanted his platoon joined together in the village before he confronted a force his size or larger.

The night was pitch-black. We stopped shooting illumination because when everyone is moving at night it can be useless or even counterproductive.

We were trying to keep up with the action from the CP. Lou called his outstanding patrols. "Mike 2-1, this is Mike 2 Actual. We will be at the village in ten minutes. I want you to move to the west edge of the village and set up a block. I will join you there."

"Mike 2-1 Alpha [the three-man alley cat], this is Mike 2. Are you up on the situation, over?"

Already, 2-1 Alpha was on the move. When the Marine keyed his handset, he was puffing. "Roger, Mike 2. Twenty to thirty November Victor Alpha on the wire, headed north. We all meet on the west side of the village."

Now there is confusion. Someone in Lou's group sees enemy soldiers moving ahead. Marines fire and the enemy briefly goes to ground. Shortly after, they are up and moving east. Lou's unit fires again and in return receives several rounds from the darkness.

We briefly discuss on the company net the where and what. This group is estimated at only ten or twelve. If the original sighting coming from the barrier is correct, this cannot be the same bunch. We decide this must be a second, smaller group. Lou wants his platoon back together and decides to continue to the village and intercept the larger enemy force rather than break off to chase this one.

Lou calls his two patrols. "Mike 2-1, this is Mike 2. What is your poz [position]? Over."

"Two, this is 2-1. We are in place. Over."

Next Lou calls the three-man fire team. "2-1 Alpha, this is 2. There is more than one group of Charlie out here. Keep your eyes open. Over."

From 2-1 Alpha comes an almost jovial "Get some!" Fateful words.

Three or four minutes pass in silence, then a firefight erupts somewhere between the hill and the village.

AK-47 and M-16 rifle fire, an M-79 (40mm grenade launcher), more rifles, then hand grenades, more rifles, then more grenades. Then silence.

Lou's voice quickly breaks through. "2-1 Alpha, this is Mike 2. Over."

No answer. "2-1 Alpha, this is Mike 2. Over." Still no answer. "Mike 2-1 Alpha, this is Mike 2. If you can hear me, key your handset. Over." No sound breaks the net.

Several minutes pass as Lou and the skipper discuss the situation. Someone suggests that the radio might be hit and 2-1 Alpha cannot transmit. But as the minutes pass they would have time to fire a flare or find some way to communicate. Still no response. 2-1 Alpha is gone.

2d Platoon searched all night for their lost alley cat. We shot illumination to provide light, but 2d Platoon found nothing. At first light the rest of Mike Company joined in to sweep the paddies and trees, looking for our comrades. It was a somber task and no one had any illusions as to what we would find. It was 1000 when the radio crackled with word that they had been found.

Instead of following the elliptical tree line east and then south around to the village, they had cut across 250 meters of open paddy. The three bodies were found about forty meters short of the tree line. They had reached that point when the large group of NVA either took them under fire or perhaps came busting out of the woods in front of them. Thirty men moving fast against three; it was a short fight.

The bodies were next to a low paddy dike and had been jammed or stomped down into the mud to make them more difficult to find. Indeed, 2d Platoon had swept the area twice under illumination, but had not seen them. Two of the bodies were stacked, indicating that one Marine wounded was being dragged or carried by another when they were killed. The third body was about five feet away. Parts of their bodies appeared to be missing, but in the mud and water it was hard to tell.

Someone had either used the captured 40mm grenade launcher to blast each head or had placed a grenade under each head. In either case the explosions had blasted away any recognizable features. The three were wearing their dog tags, so we were able to identify them. In addition to three lives, we had lost an M-79, a radio, and two M-16s.

Mutilation is not uncommon in combat. Mike Company was known to take ears at times. A squad leader told me, "Once you've killed a man, there is not much else you can do to hurt him, Lieutenant. But sometimes these new guys think we are fighting ghosts. Having that ear in your pocket is reassurance that Charlie is flesh and blood, too. If you get a little edgy at night, you can reach in your pocket and squeeze that ear. It helps." Like most COs in Vietnam, Captain Van Riper had issued standing orders against mutilation. Sometimes officers know only what the troops want them to know.

Even though it went on both ways, and even though everyone knew what to expect, losing three popular Marines that way hit Mike Company hard.

For the next few days the company was in a funk. I had known only one of the Marines who died. One had been in-country only a few days, and one was in the middle of his tour. The third had completed a thirteen-month tour and extended, or "re-upped," for an additional six months.

In return for extending your tour, the Department of

Defense would fly you anywhere they fly, and that was anywhere in the free world, for thirty days, for free. Throughout the early years of the war, extending was a very popular idea. The war was such that hundreds if not thousands of Americans extended again and again. Guys went everywhere, of course. Bangkok was popular, as was Hong Kong. Many went to Europe and a few even went home. This one had gone to Australia.

With a month in Sydney, he of course fell in love. Christmas night was his first patrol since arriving back the night before. He spent Christmas day telling anyone who would listen about going back to Australia when he got out of the Corps.

Maybe it was just a coincidence, but no matter where I traveled for the rest of my tour, I never heard anyone mention extending again. While the war was still *the* place to be for a lifer, for the rest of us the war had begun to turn sour. Everyone knew it would end soon, anyway.

New Year's Eve, December 31, 1968. The week had been almost quiet. The Tet holidays were approaching, and it was already being referred to as Tet II. The enemy was moving larger numbers of troops, but contact was not up significantly. At about 1400 hours we heard shouting in the lines. A Vietnamese male had been spotted four hundred meters out, casually strolling our way on the web of paddy dikes south of the hill. A Marine was in the lines with a scope.

The word was quick: "Don't shoot. We want him. Put a glass on him. Don't lose him." The suspect strolled along for another minute or two and then suddenly seemed to become self-aware. He began to look around

as if to see if he were alone. I cannot believe he was unaware that two hundred Marines were staring right
down on him. He suddenly dropped on his stomach, slid
into the water, and disappeared. The closest patrol was
through a tree line five hundred meters east. It would
take them fifteen or twenty minutes to arrive. No need
to hurry. But when they finally did arrive, we were unable to talk them to the right spot.

It was really a web of dikes, and the patrol got close
but became confused by our instructions. For what
seemed like several frustrating minutes we were talking
to each other, but there was no communication. The patrol included two or three Vietnamese Rangers. With
Marines from the hill beginning to shout instructions
across four hundred meters of paddies, one of our
Rangers got one of their Rangers on the radio and spoke
six or seven words into the handset. The other Ranger
did not even respond. He handed the handset back to
the Marine and walked directly to the spot we had fixed.
He knelt down, reached into the water, and pulled the
VC out of the water by his hair.

I am sure there is a simple explanation, but it was
quite a surprise to all the Americans standing around
slack-jawed. The patrol brought the POW back to the
hill, and he was turned over to the Rangers for interrogation.

At 2000 that evening, it was quiet. All the patrols and
ambushes were in place for the night, but it would be
another couple of hours before any action would begin
in our TAOR. We were hanging in our hooch when a
captain whom no one recognized came to visit Captain
Van Riper. He stayed only fifteen or twenty minutes. As

he left, we engaged him; yes, he knew that the Rangers were questioning the VC.

"How are they questioning him?" someone asked.

He looked very official and said, "I really don't know. No American personnel are present at the questioning. If I were to guess, I might say soap in a sock, or maybe just a nightstick."

I do not know how long they questioned him, but about two hours later we heard that the young man had confessed his sins and repatriated. And, yes, there was a mortar buried in a bunker. And there were two VC with the mortar. And the three of them were planning to shoot the mortar at Hill 10.

If you had asked me, I'd have said let them shoot. With very little effort we could have had one or more of Golf Battery's howitzers pointing right down at the village, a thousand meters away. Anyone lobbing mortar rounds at us would meet with grief. But I was just the FO and nobody asked me.

Bright and early New Year's Day, Mike Company saddled up along with our platoon of Rangers. The prisoner would show us the mortar.

As we lined up along the main road through camp, it was obvious that our newest patriot had not come back over easily. Fourteen or fifteen years old, he was wearing black pajamas, a shirt with one button buttoned, and no shoes. His face was swollen, lumpy, and discolored. Both eyes were swollen shut and his lips were balloon-like. His right arm was clasped tightly to his side and across his stomach. His left arm hung limply at his side. As we pushed off in a column of twos on the road east out of camp, he could not stand straight and could not really walk. He had to shuffle to keep up.

John Mason's platoon went off the hill due south to act as a blocking force to the west and south of the village. We moved east to the main road and then south for twenty or thirty minutes. When we turned west, back toward the village, Lee Neely's 1st Platoon split north to block that exit. As we entered the village, most of Lou Piatt's 2d Platoon dropped off to close the circle. Seven or eight of us were in company headquarters, plus Lou and a dozen Rangers. We entered the village from the east, led by our newest patriot, who was being held by the neck.

Fifteen or twenty thatched hooches were scattered around an area about one hundred by two hundred meters. A few of the hooches were clustered together, but most seemed to be set around randomly, with a couple of large open areas separating the structures. Some of the Rangers poked into several hooches as the rest of us proceeded directly to a hooch on the west side of the village.

The hooch in question was typical of most others. Adjoining the front door was a ten-by-ten-foot thatched cover raised about seven feet high by four poles. It provided welcome shade just in front of the hooch itself. On the north side of the shade was a dirt bunker. On the west side was the hooch, and the south side had a thatched wall or divider standing between two of the poles. The only completely open side was to the east.

As I walk up, Marines and Rangers are milling around the hooch and the bunker. Someone with a flashlight has checked in the bunker and found nothing. Now a Ranger is in the shade, next to the hooch, digging into the side of the bunker with an E-tool (entrenching tool). I head for the other side of the shade, drop my pack, and sit down on it, my back to the thatched wall. Eight or ten feet in front of me, the Ranger interpreter is watching the progress of the digging. The E-tool scrapes the dirt from a place where two vertical thatched mats come together like walls to make a corner.

I drop my helmet between my feet and look down as the interpreter sticks his K-bar between the mats and pries them apart. As he leans down to peer inside between the mats, the muzzle of an AK-47 pokes out and fires twice into his face.

The sound in that small space is ear-splitting. My head snaps up in time to see the interpreter's body jerk straight up and collapse backward. Several voices scream "Grenade!" I have my helmet on and move to my left, around the end of the thatched wall, when the first explosion comes. I do a short U-turn to my left and stop on the other side of the thatch. Immediately there are two more explosions. I look over my left shoulder as a Ranger pushes our POW toward me and takes off in the other direction, toward a pile of dirt. I reach back and grab the kid by his arm and pull my pistol with my right hand. Suddenly M-16s are firing from behind the mat. Bullets are snapping through the mat and flying in several directions.

From my right, twenty feet away, a Vietnamese male wearing black pajama pants and a loud red, green, and blue Hawaiian shirt lopes out of the bunker area I have just vacated. He is yelling back over his shoulder and swinging the AK-47 at his side. I cock my .45 and, still holding the prisoner with my left hand, fire two quick shots with my right. His head snaps in my direction and the AK points at me. My .45, firing directly at him from twenty feet away, must sound like a cannon.

I am looking down the AK's muzzle as I fire a third shot and then a fourth. Either his rifle misfires or he decides I am no threat to his safety. He continues to lope along without breaking stride. (Five years later I had dinner with Lou Piatt in Los Angeles, and he was still kidding me about my poor pistol marksmanship.)

Two riflemen and my scout-observer run up beside me and begin to fire from the standing offhand position. Each fires several shots, but the VC continues running toward the tree line a hundred meters away. Finally my scout drops to the kneeling position and aims. The escaping VC is eighty meters away when the scout fires. With his right foot in the air, the VC does a pirouette on his left heel. As his body spins around to face us, the company guide fires a tracer bullet that, we all see, hits the VC in the navel. He drops like a sack of wheat across a paddy dike.

I step back several steps and look around the mat to see what else is happening. A Marine runs up on top of a low mound of dirt about thirty feet north of the bunker. He fires a full magazine into the second, already dead, VC. I look back toward the first downed VC. A Marine comes out of the trees from twenty meters beyond with his pistol drawn. He walks over to the VC, pumps one bullet into his head, and the chase is over.

Had the two VC thrown three American M-26 hand grenades, we would have had someone dead and ten or fifteen wounded. Three grenades in such a small area with that many exposed troops spells disaster. But these two had thrown Chi-Com (Chinese Communist) grenades—

homemade and unpredictable. These Chi-Coms had made a lot of noise but caused only four wounded casualties.

The two dead VC were brothers, ages seventeen and fifteen. Plenty old enough. The mortar was there, too, so the young POW would go to Da Nang for repatriation.

I walked with my scout and radio operator out across the paddy to the first body. My scout was really pumped up about getting his first confirmed kill. He had made his bones. Like big game hunters, we each put one foot on the dike and had a group picture taken with the kill.

We turned to walk back to the CP and found a big problem. Word had spread that the interpreter had been killed and the Vietnamese Rangers were going berserk in retaliation.

Flames were already rising from several hooches, and the Rangers were beating, stomping, and butt-whipping every civilian in sight. Captain Van Riper was yelling at the Vietnamese platoon commander, and the Ranger was screaming back at the top of his voice. The two soldiers were only a foot apart, waving their arms and shouting at each other in two different languages. I still have pictures of the burning hooches in a scrapbook.

A medevac arrived quickly and took the casualties to Da Nang. Marines were wetting towels and trying to put out fires where they could, but the Rangers' rampage ran for several minutes. No shots were fired, and I do not think anyone was killed. It may be that they simply ran out of people to beat.

We found another bad problem. We had also killed one of our own. John Mason's platoon was strung out in the tree line we had fired toward. When the shooting started, they had all hit the deck. When the company re-formed,

John was one man short. A search found him—with an M-16 wound to his chest. He had never made a sound.

The medevac chopper left with one dead Marine, one dead Ranger, and four wounded Marines, including Gunny Gregory. I do not know what happened to the two dead VC; we might have left them there. Shortly after, word came to pull out, so we started moving north. As we left the village, we formed two columns to avoid the mines.

At the north edge of the village was an old mamma-san in black pajamas sitting on the ground, slumped back against a banana tree. She had been beaten half to death and blood was trickling from her nose. Her breathing was harsh and labored. She appeared only semiconscious and her legs were splayed out, lying across the trail. Each Marine had to step over her legs as he passed. Most stepped lightly, without looking down. I would have, too, but as I approached she slid further to her right side and slumped even further down. Her breathing stopped. Her white hair, once pulled back in a neat bun, was now loose and askew. After a hesitation her ragged breathing continued, and then I, too, stepped over her and made my way back to the hill with Mike Company.

I had been feeling exhilarated. Now I felt dirty. It would have been easy to feel like an authentic oppressor at the time. I had to force any thoughts or doubts to the very back of my mind: If I survive and rotate, then someday I will sit down and think about all this, but not today. It is too dangerous to think today. Just do your job and try to keep up.

For the next two weeks the pace was pretty fast. At least one of the companies was in contact each night, but the enemy was still moving. He would not stand and fight. We all expected that attitude to change soon with the approach of the Tet holiday.

After four or five days, Gunny Gregory returned from Da Nang. He was all patched up and still full of fight. He did take a bit of ribbing about having all four wounds on his back half. But he had a plausible explanation that somehow left him still fighting the enemy when the wounds occurred.

While no one else remembered it quite that way, he stuck to his story, and he was, after all, the gunny. He was also "short" (nearing the end of his tour of duty), so he turned around in two days and headed to Da Nang on his way back to the World.

His replacement was Gunny Haywood. The new company gunny quickly proved to be competent and motivated, and the company ran well with him as a ramrod. Still, I am sure that we all missed having Gunny Gregory's personality around.

We talked constantly about what was going on each day, happenings in the company and in the battalion, but I do not remember dwelling on any of it. The war was very much up in my face. The dead, the wounded, and those who rotated were somewhere else, and we were still here, fighting the war. There is not time in the midst of an ongoing cataclysm to stop and reminisce. The gone are gone; the war goes on. Stay alert.

During the last two weeks of January, I had a surprise. My good friend Gene Gray showed up at Mike Company. Gene was a very bright and resourceful guy from Idaho. He had had the bunk next to me at OCS, and we went through Basic School and artillery school together. After Fort Sill, Gene went to a language school and was

just now arriving in-country. Another surprise: Gene
Gray was my replacement.

Most new FOs expected to spend six months in the
bush and then rotate to either a 105 battery or back to
11th Marines in Da Nang. This seemed to mean that I
would spend only four months in the bush. I was not
disappointed. When I first arrived in Vietnam, I had
wanted to be in a firefight. By this point I had been in
several. I gladly would have gone home if they'd needed
the room. Instead, I was to become the battalion FSC for
3/7. I would be on the battalion staff and work for Lieutenant Colonel Quinn. I had one day to brief Gene on
the FO's job, and then I officially transferred to battalion staff.

In this case, "transfer" meant humping my gear fifty
meters up the hill to the battalion staff hooch. While my
gear would be in the staff hooch, my body would be
across the road in the battalion CP—about twenty
hours of every day.

The FSC job gave the term "full-time" a whole new
meaning. I slept in the CP, ate many of my meals there,
and never allowed myself to be more than thirty seconds
away from the radios at any time. On Hill 10 the FSC
job kept you in "the bunker."

Any weapon larger than a 60mm mortar, including
naval gunfire and air support, that fired in or into 3/7's
TAOR had to be cleared first by the FSC. As an FO, I
had shot and adjusted naval guns, and it was always exciting, even if we did not have a real target. But the FSC
job consisted of clearing target grids, which were eight-
digit numbers that related to some map location. The
job just amounted to dealing with one set of numbers
after another. It would have been the most mundane of

jobs, except that I had learned the hard way that lives were at stake on every call.

The new job quickly developed a rhythm. My day actually began at about 1300. I would coordinate with the FOs from each of my four rifle companies, and either collect or assign H&I fires for the TAOR. Then I sent this information to 11th Marines. Some of those targets were shot by Golf Battery and some by the battalion's 81mm mortars. Each afternoon we would receive targets from 11th Marines for us to clear. Those targets would be shot by division's firepower, the 155s or 8-inchers from Da Nang. Sometimes we even got naval gunfire.

Before dark the FOs shot in any targets they wanted for that night. Then the evening rocked along until 2200, when the first H&I fires began. Often sometime just before that or soon thereafter, one of the battalion's infantry units would make enemy contact. Then the radios would fill the night with excited conversations and strings of numbers. FOs would call for illumination or blocking fires. The artillery would begin to shoot, and back in the bunker we would anxiously follow it all. We listened between the artillery radios and the infantry radios, and tried to keep in touch with the FOs when troops were moving around.

It grew quiet at times, and a bunk was available in the CP for me to take catnaps. However, a radioman was always on duty, ready to shake me awake if necessary.

The day for the rest of battalion staff began with the morning staff meeting at 0800. Each section gave a brief presentation to Lieutenant Colonel Quinn about activities in the past twenty-four hours and current plans for the next twenty-four. By 0830 the meeting ended, and my day ended with it. I would walk across the road to the staff hooch and crash until 1300, when it all began again.

I liked Quinn. About five feet nine inches tall with a thinning flattop, he was stocky with a round face and the neck of a bull. He had joined the Marine Corps as a private during World War II and made several island landings. He had fought in Korea and along the way earned a commission. The colonel had a ready smile and a kindly manner toward his troops, including me, but the infantry commander in him was always close to the surface.

Although contact with the enemy seemed strong and growing, almost all the fighting was at night. We knew that would change, too.

Waiting for Tet II was like waiting for the other shoe to drop. The enemy was moving his troops and storing his supplies. At some point he would stand and fight, and we expected he would fight until he ran out of men and supplies. Then the survivors would go to ground and back to the old way of fighting. I had been on the job for a couple of weeks or so when it finally hit the fan.

It was late morning and I was crashed in the staff hooch when shooting started to the north of the hill. From the direction, I knew it had to be one of my units. By the time I got my trousers on, boots laced, and crossed the road to the CP, we heard shooting to the west. That had to be Lima Company. For the next several days—and at the time it seemed to last forever—we sustained daytime contact with the enemy somewhere in our TAOR every day.

As long as the NVA was willing to stand and fight, the Three-F Principle was definitely in effect. The radioed voices that came to us from every direction ran high with excitement: "Fire mission! Enemy in the open! Look at them! Look at them!"

Every company in the battalion took casualties. I do not remember the numbers, but we had several dozen casualties, dead and wounded. At the time the losses seemed overshadowed by the kills we were getting.

Day after day, 3/7 was rocking and rolling. In one action, Kilo killed thirty enemy with no Marines dead and only a few minor wounds.

Mike Company had an all-day fight in which Lou Piatt earned his Navy Cross. When his platoon became pinned down, Lou crawled forward under fire and flanked the enemy ambush. He killed six NVA, took out a machine gun, and saved his platoon.

Lima Company killed more than a dozen, including a Chinese or North Korean officer wearing a distinctive khaki uniform. Because neither the Chinese nor Koreans can teach the Vietnamese anything about fighting, he must have been a student and not an adviser. But at the time, the FOs were certain we had uncovered an international conspiracy.

Aside from the numbers that came in from each rifle company, we discovered a mass grave that contained between sixty and eighty NVA bodies. Most had been stripped of their uniforms and were barely covered by a thin layer of dirt. The bodies appeared to have been gathered from the nearby surrounding area, and the cause of death in all cases appeared to be shrapnel wounds. There were no bomb craters around and nothing like enough artillery craters to have done so much damage. The dead may have been killed by artillery with proximity fuses (which detonate in the air) or a luckily placed COFRAM bomb (controlled fragmentation munitions—a bomb that drops dozens of small explosives). But they had been there for several days in the sun, and the scene was ripe. The bodies were thoroughly decayed; very little flesh remained, except for the buttocks. Word of the find flashed through the battalion, giving truth to the old saying "When you lose your ass, you've lost it all."

The morning staff meetings were enthusiastic. The numbers were good and every day seemed to bring more good news. It would have been a good time except, with all that was happening, the battalion was tense and the pressure was terrific. At one point I almost came to blows with the battalion S-3 (operations officer).

The CP was a hardened bunker about twenty-five feet square. My post was in the northwest corner. I sat against the west wall and to my right sat my radioman. We had wooden chairs and a wooden desk with the radios, codebooks, and other paraphernalia sitting on top. In the southeast corner of the room were the infantry's radios.

One afternoon several days after the daytime action had begun, the quiet around me was broken by Gene Gray's voice squawking out of the radio, "Check fire, check fire! Someone is shooting tanks at us. Turn it off! Turn it off!" Through the noise and confusion he could not initially tell from which direction he was taking fire. Almost immediately Mike Company's radio across the room began to call out, "Check fire. Check fire!"

The S-3, a captain, was a giant. He must have been an offensive lineman in college. He was standing facing his radios, and then he turned around in our direction and yelled, "Stop your artillery. You are shooting Mike Company."

Hill 55 memorial service, November 1968. Twelve dead, thirty-eight wounded.

Memorial service bulletin, Mike Company,
November 12, 1968.

MIKE COMPANY
THIRD BATTALION, SEVENTH MARINES
FIRST MARINE DIVISION

12 NOVEMBER 1968
* *

IN MEMORIAM

D. B. HENDERSON	4 November 1968
E. G. ANDERSON	4 November 1968
R. G. SKAGGS	6 November 1968
G. C. MULLIN	6 November 1968
G. R. PETERSON	6 November 1968
E. D. HENRY	6 November 1968
D. B. SLEIGH 2/Lt	6 November 1968
J. M. TIMMONS	6 November 1968
W. G. CAMP	6 November 1968
R. SOLER	6 November 1968
P. D. ENGLISH	7 November 1968
A. L. HARVIN	6 NOVEMBER '68

These our brothers we commend to the mercy of
Almighty God, praying that He will comfort with his
presence those who are left behind.
* *

INVOCATION

ROLL CALL

PLACING OF HELMET

PLACING OF NEW TESTAMENT

SCRIPTURE READINGS

LORD'S PRAYER

HYMN "O GOD OUR HELP IN AGES PAST"

MEDITATION

Left to right: John Mason, Terry Williamson, Capt. Paul
Van Riper, and Bill Hardwick.

Mason and Hardwick with Lou Piatt.

Seated left to right: FO Scout with binoculars, Hardwick with phone, and Lt. Tom Harrell looking, along with Capt. Van Riper (standing, right) at Hill 10.

Looking west across the rocket belt: double concertina on two sides of a killing zone.

Life in the rocket belt.

During the sixty-one days from November 15, 1968, through January 15, 1969, Mike Company lost fifty-seven legs, "a leg a day."

After a few days, the pilots knew where they were going.

Though we had the best of intentions, dealing with civilians was sometimes awkward.

In the rocket belt, one dead Marine, one dead Ranger, and two dead VC made the NPF (National Police Force) go berserk.

"Arizona," May–July 1969.

Resupply choppers came almost every other day.

FAC party local: Capt. Joe Fluett (center, without shirt)—"navel" officer; Hardwick (right, with shirt); Al Thayer (with shades); and two unidentified soldiers.

Profit motive—with no cars to wash, what's the next dirtiest thing?

Be it ever so humble . . . seeking shade where there is none.

By the time I left "Arizona," my morale could no longer transcend the food.

For some Marines, becoming RTO was reward for walking point for six months.

First light—we had spent all night on the Hot Dog, and the gunny cut a pole to carry our dead.

Getting short—back at An Hoa things were quiet.

Unsung heroes of the war (AO) in an OV-10 Bronco.

The 8-inch howitzers were located next to the airstrip. I spent a week working on the drainage with "appropriated" material.

Hell rained down on An Hoa on a regular basis. You had either a hardened bunker or a sandbag donut close by.

On Sunday night, we ate steak.

Hardwick with a "hog," an 8-inch howitzer.

Loading up.

"Shot"—the most accurate artillery piece in the world.

My radioman and I were already working two radios, calling adjoining units, calling for check fire, and asking who had tanks firing. I don't know what the S-3 thought we were doing, but since he was behind the curve and we were in the midst of a crisis, I ignored him and kept talking on my handset.

The S-3 strode across the room as Mike's radioman spoke again, "It is tanks. Across the river." By the time the S-3 reached my desk he was yelling, "Stop the tanks! You're killing Marines! You're killing Marines!"

We would have been scrambling for any Marine unit in trouble, but this was Mike Company. I still considered Mike to be *my* company. I was desperately trying to hear the words coming from my handset, and as the S-3 approached, still shouting, I reached back with my right hand and gave him a shove. I turned to my right and yelled, "Get the fuck out of my face!"

I realized immediately I had made a bad mistake. The S-3 captain was enormous. He lunged at me with his arms outstretched, his face bright red, and eyes almost bulging. He reached over the radioman and grabbed me by my shirt. Even though I am six feet tall and at the time weighed about 175 pounds, he lifted me out of my chair by my camouflage blouse and began to pull me out into the room. The radioman was caught between us and was thrashing like a bug trying to escape. I had been sitting cramped over for several hours and could not get my legs to straighten under me. There was no question that the good captain was about to pull my arms off and break my body into pieces, and I was about to take it. (Thank you, sir. May I have another?)

Fortunately, the battalion XO, a major, witnessed the entire event and was also moving fast. He jumped over to us, stuck his left arm between the captain and me, and then tried to jam his body between us. To his credit the radioman never lost his place in the codebook. From the floor he called out, "This must be it!" The captain let go and I fell across a wooden chair, scrambled back to my radio, and turned the dial. I called for a check fire and received an acknowledgment.

I looked back to my right. The XO major was holding the captain in a bear hug. He was saying soothing things to the S-3 captain and slowly pushing him away. The captain was looking back at me, still in a barely controlled rage. Our eyes locked for several uncomfortable seconds, and then Gene Gray's voice came over the radio and broke the tension. "Okay, I think you got it."

The captain turned around, and he and the major walked out of the bunker. Mike's radioman was next. "That's it, you got it."

My radioman got up, straightened his chair, and sat down. I sat in my chair and tried to regain my composure. I was feeling overwhelmed by so much happening at once, and I noticed that my whole body was trembling. I was slowly getting myself back together from what I considered a near-death experience when I looked at the Marine next to me. The poor lance corporal, caught up in the brawl among these crazy officers, was panting so hard I worried he might hyperventilate.

The room had eight or ten Marines present, but there was dead silence. Barely a minute passed before the S-3 captain returned to the bunker, alone. He crossed to the middle of the room, turned in my direction, and said, "You had better watch your ass." There was no doubt in the room as to whom he was speaking. He strode back to his radios and the watch continued, but you could have cut the tension in the air with a knife. Fortunately, Mike Company took no casualties—and neither did the battalion CP.

During my tour as FO, I was called on the carpet twice for using profanity on 3/11's radio net. The first time was the night 2d Platoon had been shot up in the graveyard in Dodge City. I had dead and wounded Marines in a firefight a thousand meters away, and it was a long, frustrating night. Sometime during it all I used the F-word on 11th Marines' net while talking to the guns in Da Nang. The next morning I received a message to stop by and see the battalion commander of 3/11. Profanity on the radio net is a big deal in the Marine Corps. On Hill 55, 3/11's CP was conveniently located next door to the 7th Marines CP.

The lieutenant colonel was quite pleasant. He asked how Mike had done the night before, even though he already knew. He assured me I was doing a good job and even made a kind of joke about how sensitive the commandant is to profanity on the net. We both laughed, and I promised not to do it again.

The next time was barely a week after we had moved to Hill 10. We were still learning our way around the new TAOR. I was with a platoon about fifteen hundred meters east of the hill. During late afternoon we came under fire from a rifle and a light automatic weapon. Because it was late, we decided to hunker down rather than pursue. Before it grew dark I wanted to shoot in at least three targets for the night. I really enjoyed shooting Golf Battery, and everything had always been quick and smooth. The standard procedure was to adjust single rounds onto a target, and then the FDC (fire direction center) would read back a target designation with a letter and three numbers, such as Alpha 101. If there was trouble that night, you could call for rounds on Alpha 101 or Alpha 103, and even in the dark everyone knew what to expect.

That night they read back the target designation and also the eight-digit map coordinate. This was a different procedure. Their radioman said something about keeping the numbers together for safety. It did not make sense to me at the time, but in the bush we seldom knew what was going on.

It all became clear later that night when we got into a fight. I called Golf Battery and told them to shoot Alpha 103, but the radioman there said he could not shoot until I read back to him the corresponding eight-digit coordinate. I told him I did not have the eight-digit coordinate, but that I did have contact with the enemy and he should start shooting, now.

Next came a different voice on the radio. He patiently explained that for safety reasons I would be required to read back both the target designation and the corresponding eight-digit grid. (Forget that if you have the eight-digit coordinate you do not *need* a target designation!)

I shot back a brilliant plume of profanity into the handset, explaining that it was dark "out here" and that in the midst of a firefight I was not going to turn on a flashlight to read extra digits back to someone of questionable parentage when he had both a light and all the digits right in front of him. I ended the tirade with the assurance that if he didn't start shooting immediately, I would hike back to the hill and shove a plotting table up his ass.

It was way too much, but we were being shot at and I was pissed. What I received back on my radio was a teeth-clenched "Roger. Out." Golf began shooting almost immediately. Each time I adjusted fire, they read me back an eight-digit grid, and each time I gave them a very polite "Thank you."

The next day back on Hill 10, I received word to stop in and say hello to the battalion commander of 3/11. To my great relief, it was a different lieutenant colonel. Vietnam was good for turnover if not much else. The colonel was pleasant and asked me what had happened. I explained to him that I was in a firefight at night and that I had been unaware of a change in procedure until then. I could not turn on a light without first pulling out a poncho (to cover and obscure the light), and I lost my temper at the change. The colonel said he understood my situation, but that recently grids had gotten separated from target designations, and wrong grids had been fired.

I readily agreed with the colonel that safety had to be a top priority. I suggested that it was difficult enough for an FO to operate at night, especially under fire, and that if there was a problem in the FDC keeping grids and target designations together, the problem might best be addressed in the FDC, where there is light and no one is dodging bullets. I added, "If I have the eight-digit coordinate, why do I need a target number?"

To my surprise and great relief, the colonel agreed. After some discussion, he said, "Perhaps we need more thought before changing field procedures for the FOs." I promised him that I would never use profanity on his net again, and for the rest of my tour, wherever I went, I was careful.

I found that throughout my service, my superior officers were fair and courteous to me. In Vietnam, I found that the Marine Corps *did* operate like a team. Not only my superiors but most of the Marines I met and dealt with were normally helpful and positive. It was a good feeling.

But now I'd had this incident with the captain in the CP. I was glad the XO had been present. I felt the S-3 had crossed the line. We were doing everything we could to stop the fire, and he had caused confusion. I could not operate with him yelling in my ear. Still, I half expected military policemen to march through the door at any moment and chain me upside down in some brig. I must have been right, though, because the issue was dropped.

The next morning after the staff meeting, Lieutenant Colonel Quinn stopped me and asked, "How are you doing? Everything okay?"

I said, "Yes, sir. Absolutely."

He grinned at me and said, "Hang in there." Needless to say, my relationship with the S-3 was chilly after that.

Tet II had a specific beginning in my part of the war, but I do not remember any real ending. I was the FSC of 3/7 from the middle of January until the middle of March 1969. On a slow day there was plenty to do; on a busy day it became an incredible grind. One day in the middle of March, I was called to see Lieutenant Colonel Quinn.

I walked into his office, and the first thing he said was, "When did you become a FAC?" I had been so focused on grid coordinates, unit names, and frequencies for so long that when I heard the term "FAC," my mind went blank. It was like hearing a language from another life-time.

He continued, "I did not even know the Corps cross-trained artillery officers as forward air controllers. It is probably a good idea. In any event, you are headed to An Hoa to be a forward air controller for 5th Marines."

I walked out of Quinn's office still soaking in the sudden change. Forward air controller. An Hoa. Where *is* An Hoa? Who cares? After eight weeks as FSC, I had begun to feel like one of the mole people. Sunlight made me squint, and I could see how one might develop feelings of isolation in this job. It is one of the most intense things I have ever done.

I heard no reports of Americans being killed by friendly fire on my watch. If that is true, it is due as much to luck as to skill. If it is not true, I might be the last to know.

We got a report that one of our mortar rounds had killed two civilian farmers. When Tet II began, the curfew for civilians was changed from 2200 to 2000. On the first night of Tet II, we killed the two farmers with the first H&I round we fired. I simply went back to the 2200 program.

"In any event," as the colonel had said, I was headed for 5th Marines. I would be out of the bunker and back in the war. I felt good. I felt *released*. I briefed my replacement that afternoon and stood watch with him that night. The next morning I caught a chopper to An Hoa.

Be careful what you wish for.

4

A Misuse of Power

It was my view from Paris [in January 1972] that we
would be better to take the peace agreement we had
[with the same terms available in 1969] and try to enforce an imperfect document, than to continue fighting
for several more months while trying to improve the
terms.
                                —DR. HENRY KISSINGER,
                    Congressional POW hearings, June 1992

Willie, Willie, what the hell are we doing here, Willie?
                    —LT. JOHN JURACEK, Liberty Bridge, 1969

I never knew if there was an original village of An
Hoa. I had no inclination for sightseeing. An Hoa, the
firebase, seemed to be about one mile square of wire, fortifications, weapons, and defenses. It was located about
thirty miles southwest of Da Nang on the east side of a
river, the Song Tinh Yen. The north, west, and south
perimeter lines of the base were strung with wire. On the
east was an airstrip along with 155mm and 8-inch howitzers. In the northwest corner sat a 105 battery.

Most of An Hoa's structures were squat, hardened,
sandbagged bunkers. Any structure that was not hardened had a deep foxhole, or several, close by. Hell rained
down on An Hoa on a regular basis.

The enemy had 122mm and 140mm rockets as well as
large mortars and a 120mm recoilless rifle, and he fired
them all at the base and the airstrip whenever he

pleased. This was no Khe Sanh, but unlike Da Nang, which was on the coast and had a defensive belt around it, An Hoa was inland, right next to the enemy's supply line. He had lots of ordance to expend.

I checked into 5th Marines CP, and there was John Juracek. We had a great reunion and caught up on news from home and any word of friends. Jim Harvey had been in a battery that was overrun and suffered 50 percent casualties. Jim had survived and was now a FAC for another regiment.

John had arrived the previous afternoon and knew something of our new assignment. We would not be staying in An Hoa. I was about to feel good that we would not be living in a bull's-eye. Then he told me that we would instead be going to an outpost called Liberty Bridge.

We spent that evening at the 105 battery talking to some Marines John knew. They briefed us on some of the fighting going on in the area. Liberty Bridge was being referred to as "the country club."

"It hasn't been hit in a month, and hasn't been overrun in almost three, so you're probably due."

It seemed that the occasional incoming round at An Hoa represented the biggest single concern there. Being hit by incoming was luck of the draw, almost like the mines. The 122mm rocket was the gravest concern; it could penetrate any bunker or reinforcement you could pull together. The 140mm rocket, the big mortar, and the recoilless rifle killed and maimed many Marines, but you did not want to draw a 122. In the spring of 1969, I thought An Hoa was an anxious, scary place to be. But John and I were headed for the country club.

Liberty Bridge, about eight miles east of An Hoa, was

the first bridge on the only landline joining An Hoa and 5th Marines to Da Nang.

Each day armored convoys ran the road carrying troops, rations, ammunition, and equipment back and forth in the continuous movement of war. That next morning, John and I caught a ride on the convoy headed toward Da Nang.

The first stop on the trip between An Hoa and Da Nang is Liberty Bridge. We arrived at the country club in a swirling vortex of dust and dirt and dropped our gear. As the convoy roared off and the dust began to settle, a captain approached and shook our hands. We were expected, and he was genuinely happy to see us. The captain was the FAC party leader and would be our boss.

By this point in the war I had stopped learning people's names. Somehow it was easier for me if I didn't know their names. In his real life, the captain was a navigator on an A-6 Intruder. He was a mustang (enlisted man bumped up to officer). He loved his aircraft—he could cite you a list of flaws, but he loved his plane and he loved his job. For the last two months he had been grounded.

As FAC party leader, the captain was stuck at Liberty Bridge with an experimental black box called the "beacon." He controlled the dropping of much of the unexpended ordnance returning from sorties all over the I Corps Military Region. By himself, he had been controlling the drop of more than a million pounds of bombs per month. He was quite proud of his record, and almost exhausted. It was a twenty-four-hour-a-day job.

The Department of Defense had built a gigantic supply pipeline halfway around the world. It continued to deliver millions of pounds of supplies and ordnance every month. Because it was deemed unsafe for an aircraft to land with explosives on board, any unexpended bombs were dumped in the ocean. Someone along the line must have decided to give the taxpayer more bang for his buck, so air controllers began to divert this unexpended ordnance to Liberty Bridge.

The "beacon" was a transmitter, a six-by-six-by-twelve-inch rectangular box with a stubby, tubelike antenna about one inch in diameter and eight inches high. The beacon emitted a pulse that could be received by the A-6. Using an azimuth from the beacon (a surveyed point) and a distance in linear feet, the A-6 computer could drop its load as directed. We received all kinds of aircraft, and many of the drops were on visual targets, but by far our most consistent customer was the A-6.

For our purposes, the A-6 carried twenty-six 500-pound bombs, and the crew could drop them anyway they wanted.

We usually dropped a marking bomb, then a bracket bomb, and then the remaining "stick" of twenty-four was dropped in between the two marking bombs.

Good weather and bad, day and night, the pipeline pumped out ordnance and the planes had to take off. When the weather was good, we got a bunch of odds and ends. When the weather was bad, especially up north, we would have aircraft with full loads backed up as at a busy airport. John and I would share the job the captain had been doing alone.

Liberty Bridge was headquarters for 1st Battalion, 5th Marines. They rotated companies: one company on the hill, and three companies out doing aggressive patrolling. Our defensive perimeter was up from the west end of the bridge. It ran on both sides of the road from the bridge on our east, one hundred meters up the hill to the battalion CP, and then one hundred meters beyond that to the west end of the wire. The road ran east and west and split the long axis of our defenses. On the north side of the road the defensive line was long and narrow, only seventy-five to one hundred feet deep. The 105 battery was on the north side of the road, directly across from the battalion CP. In places, the defensive wire ran right next to their gun emplacements.

The terrain there to the north sloped down and away five hundred meters to a tree line, a small village, and the westward leg of the river coming from An Hoa. There was more room on the south side of the road. Several fingers ran out and down the hill, which pushed the wire out a couple hundred feet. Aside from the artillery's bunkers, almost all the positions and structures on the hill were to the south of the road.

The battalion CP sat about fifty feet back from the road, in about the middle of the camp. Immediately south, only twenty-five feet away, was the staff hooch where John and I would bunk. About sixty feet west was the battalion sick bay. South of the staff hooch about seventy-five feet was the mess hall. Just east was another bunker and enough troop tents to sleep whoever was on the hill that night. The hill's electricity was powered by three small generators. It was not a very big place.

South and east of the mess hall the hill sloped down and away on several fingers almost one thousand meters to the edge of the free-fire zone. All unexpended ordnance had to be dropped in the free-fire zone.

The free-fire zone was three to four thousand meters across north to south, and six to seven thousand meters long east to west. The river defined the northern boundary. The eastern boundary was about as far as we could see with the ship's glass. The southern boundary was somewhat vague, so we stayed back from the vegetation line. In all, the zone was an area of about twenty square kilometers. It was truly a no-man's-land, suffering a million pounds of high explosives each month, and it looked like the moon.

We would soon discover that in a finite area like this, the most difficult thing to find was a legitimate target. For purposes of paperwork, every drop had to have a target, so we dutifully assigned a target to each drop. Enemy bunkers were popular; you had to quantify, either four or six or whatever. Enemy trench lines were specific enough, but still a bit vague. We quickly learned that if we specified a live target, the pilots would almost jump up and down in their cockpits, so to avoid confusion or midair accidents we seldom called out live targets.

The battalion CP was a hardened bunker pretty standard for Vietnam. About twenty-five feet square, it had about seven feet of headroom—four feet of it dug into the ground and three feet of it aboveground. The top of the CP bunker was the highest point in the area. That would be our post. For protection we had a donut made of sandbags that was big enough for two men. A ship's glass mounted on a tripod gave us a good view of the entire free-fire zone.

Just twenty-five feet away, the staff hooch was a twelve-man tent with a three-foot-tall blast wall made of empty 105 ammo boxes filled with sand. These were stacked around each tent to protect against rockets and mortars. If we were really caught by surprise, they made decent fighting positions.

The tent was never full. We usually had six or seven officers there at any one time. The three regulars were John and I and the battalion surgeon, who was a navy lieutenant. Other officers rotated through for a few days at a time. Our FAC party leader spent most of his time in the battalion CP. A kind of personality cult was cooking at battalion, so John and I steered clear.

The battalion surgeon was from the Dominican Republic and not even an American citizen. He had signed a pledge to serve four years in the American military in return for permission to study medicine in America. The Department of Defense sent him to the navy and then attached him to the Marine Corps. The Marine Corps medics are navy doctors and corpsmen. He had done his residency in New York City and was a very good trauma doctor. I once saw him save a young Marine we all believed had drowned. He also had a knack for keeping the wounded alive.

Life at Liberty Bridge quickly took on a dull monotony. Breakfast was from 0700 until 0800. By 0900 we had rolled up the tent flaps to try to catch any breeze that might blow past. There was never any air in the morning; it was always still. By 1000 the sweat began rolling down my sides and the card game began. It would run all day until lights out. The game changed from time to time, but it was usually hearts, bridge, or a game called back alley bridge. It was a gentlemen's way of killing time; I never saw money wagered.

At 1200 we shifted through lunch, tag-team style, in order to keep the game going. At 1400, like a good friend, the "two o'clock breeze" made life a little more bearable. The flaps came down at dark, and options for diversion were strictly limited. It was not so much like living at a country club as it was like living on the beach on a very small island.

For John and me it was also almost that laid-back. Our standard uniform was tiger shorts, "gook boots," and soft cover (a fatigue hat). Gook boots were the ever-present rubber sandals made from old tires. We quickly achieved lifeguard tans, and we had our own private air show every day. That part of it was interesting and never became boring. Aside from living like firemen, John and I were almost oblivious to the war.

If I wanted to bathe, the river was one hundred meters down the hill. Halfway down the hill, the locals had set up a string of stalls. You could get a haircut, drop off your laundry, or buy a watch. The water in the river was not really cool, but it still felt pretty good. If you got out to the middle of the river, it was deep, the water moved fast, and it did get cold. There were always Marines in the water.

Once we were clean and dry, however, we had no way to cover the hundred meters from the river back up the hill to the staff hooch without being covered by another solid coat of dirt. A variety of vehicles ran the road back and forth, both across the bridge and up and down the hill. Each time one passed, it kicked up a large vortex of dirt that fanned out and kept everything covered with fine red dust. We tried several techniques for returning to the tent while staying clean, but nothing worked.

Periodically, Charlie floated some kind of destruction downstream toward the bridge. These intrusions were normally blown out of the water before they could do any damage. We heard stories of floats detonating under the bridge and of swimmers being shot while trying to attach explosives. I can proudly report that the enemy dared not even try to blow the bridge while John and I were on watch.

Just before we arrived at Liberty Bridge, 1/5 had experienced an ugly "fragging" incident. A disliked gunnery sergeant had created bad feelings in one of the companies. Someone sneaked by the staff hooch and threw an M-26 grenade inside to teach him a lesson. Unfortunately he was not there, but a very popular first sergeant was. The first sergeant was headed home to retirement in ten days, but the grenade killed him. Several Marines knew who threw the grenade, but no one was willing to point the finger, and as far as I know the crime was never punished.

About the only physical activity each day was the volleyball game. Soon after the breeze came in at 1400, a pickup game would start between the staff officers and the snuffies. The staff and officers had some good athletes. A couple officers had played college sports, so you would expect that we would be able to hold our own against the enlisted guys. Let me tell you, 1/5 had a bunch of horses walking patrol. It seemed that no matter who they brought to the game, the snuffies kicked our butts. They took great pride in doing it, and they did it with enthusiasm. It was athletics with no rank, and playing net was a man's game. I do not remember if they won every game, but they won anytime they wanted to.

In the middle of his tour, each Marine was allowed a seven-day leave for R&R. In the first week of April it was my turn. I had been married during my senior year of college, and back in Texas we had a new baby girl learning how to walk. There was no chance to bring the baby, but I was able to meet my wife in Hawaii, and I was sorely ready for a break.

A week in Hawaii is good under almost any circumstances. In this case it was wonderful, even luxuriant. It did not matter where we went or what we did. It was important to just be close. We rented a car for the week, but we left the hotel proper only four or five times. We drove around the island one day and shot up a roll of film.

And we had dinner with a navy couple. The wives had met on the plane to Hawaii, and by coincidence I had met this navy man on the plane over from Da Nang. Frank and Lynda Ehrle were from Dallas, and Frank was a lieutenant and a lawyer in the navy, a JAG (judge advocate general) officer in Da Nang. We all had a wonderful meal in a French restaurant, and I made a good friend.

While you can take the boy out of the war, you cannot just take the war out of the boy. During the first half of my tour I had developed two involuntary responses. After my experience with Private Timmons, I had a revulsion to yellow smoke. It has a sulphurous smell like a rotten egg. I still used the smoke grenades in combat, but I had to stay clear of the smoke. One sniff and my stomach would come right up through my throat, like a scene from *Clockwork Orange*.

While in Hawaii, I discovered the second: an aversion to mines. I found that I could not easily walk in the grass or through the shrubbery. It took a conscious effort to stick with the civilians when they took off willy-nilly, strolling across the lawn. It was a very Pavlovian response.

No matter how you do it, a week in Hawaii passes much too quickly. On the plane back to Da Nang, I got to know Frank Ehrle a little better, and he filled me in on what it was like to fight the war from Da Nang: hot showers, clean sheets, and ordering meals from a menu. His closest scrape with the war so far was when the air base took rockets. Then the power would be turned off, usually interrupting the movie or the card game. It seemed a terrible inconvenience.

As our plane descended into airspace over Vietnam, I looked out my window and saw two F-4s making loops down through the atmosphere, putting a hurt on some poor jerk. Nothing had changed in the war, except that now I was halfway done.

Back at Liberty Bridge it was hot. I am sure it was hot in Hawaii, but somehow I'd failed to notice. Back at the country club I could not help but notice. It was hot and dusty.

Business was still good. The captain had come out of mothballs to help John for the week. But our routine set in again the next day. For three or four days it seemed like old times.

Most any literature that arrived from the World was shared around the tent. But if you had already read everything twice and were tired of playing cards, there was a movie every evening.

You could tell where we fell on the distribution list by the quality of the movies we saw. Nothing was too old or too banal. One night, less than a week after I returned from R&R, John and I stopped in to see what movie had arrived. The movie that night was *Rosemary's Baby*, and we were so bored we stayed to see it.

I had not liked the movie much when I had seen it previously. On this night it rocked along okay up to the rape scene. Then the film skipped to the next scene, and several seconds passed before it clicked with the troopers that the rape scene had been edited out. Suddenly catcalls and whistling filled the tent. A few Marines began yelling profanities, and after several seconds the movie stopped and the lights came on.

Someone suggested shooting the Marine running the projector. He didn't seem too worried; he explained that he just ran the film, he didn't edit it. No one seemed satisfied. Now the whiners started. It seems that about half the troops had not seen the movie and did not know there was a rape scene to begin with, and wanted to see the rest of the movie.

The protesters would have none of it. "Goddamn it, we get shot at. The food sucks. It's hotter than a bitch. And now they're fucking with our movie. It ain't right." There was a principle involved and a point had to be made, and instantly it was—the projector started up and the lights went out. Only fifteen or twenty Marines had been there to begin with, and about half of them stomped out, still bitching and making up a longer list of complaints. John and I had been the only two officers present, and we left, too, in sympathy with the protesters. We wandered back to the hooch, trying to find some humor in our situation.

Lights went out at 2130, but it was still hot and difficult to fall asleep. At 2300 another hill, about three thousand meters northeast across the river, was hit. A firefight at night is really spectacular. We all stood outside the hooch for ten or fifteen minutes, ooohing and aaahing.

Tracer rounds come in red, yellow, and even green.

Multiple detonations and flashes erupted as a Spooky gunship worked its long red tongue of fire across the ground. A million dollars' worth of pyrotechnics is a spectacular show, if you are at a safe distance. We stood for a while and finally broke up.

Everyone went back to bed except our Dominican Republic battalion surgeon. He shuffled off in his sandals and underwear to the officers' latrine, a four-holer located thirty or forty feet away between our staff hooch and the dispensary. It was right next to one of the generators.

Maybe we had all been in the war too long. Most of us put on our trousers and boots and relocated our gear before lying back down.

The AK-47 makes a loud, sharp, vicious sound. If it is fired in your direction, you cannot tell if it is fifty feet or two hundred feet away. It is the kind of sound nightmares are made of. The first one fired that night was in our direction, and it was very close.

We were all moving at once. Everyone had a post to run to, but first we had to get out of the tent alive. John and I were bunked in the middle of the tent, but we were practiced at moving quickly out, around, and up to our sandbagged donut. As soon as we cleared the tent we saw the bright flash of a flamethrower, and the generator near the sick bay exploded in a ball of fire. Almost immediately we looked back to see the last of our tent mates still clearing the flaps when the tent exploded. It billowed upward several feet and then collapsed onto strewn cots and equipment.

The life expectancy of a flamethrower operator in combat is measured in seconds. The enemy had three flamethrowers inside the wire with us that night, one for each generator. It is a cheap way to sell your life.

John and I sat back-to-back with our two pistols and a radio. As you might imagine, we were working the radio pretty hard. Meanwhile, a major firefight was raging all around us, primarily across the road at the artillery battery.

Ours was not the only tent blown. The enemy threw many satchel charges that night. No one wanted to be inside a bunker when a satchel charge plopped down. Everyone had a fighting position to hustle for. So at the first sound of trouble, everyone moved at once. A sapper lying in front of a bunker full of sleeping cannon crews killed the first four Marines who ran out.

In the darkness it was difficult to tell the good shadows from the bad shadows—until they fired. After several minutes of close, hard fighting, two of the crews got their guns pointed down and started firing flechettes— antipersonnel rounds filled with thousands of steel darts. Fired point-blank and at a full charge-seven, they will clear the wire and everything else. The round is devastating.

We still had more than two dozen sappers inside the wire taking positions in twos and threes and fighting to the death. An artillery lieutenant led the counterattack and should have received the Medal of Honor as far as I am concerned. He did not, of course. The main medals would go to the battalion commander and one of the staff officers. To quote a local movie critic, "It ain't right."

Within ten or fifteen minutes, John and I had a Spooky gunship dropping flares and using its waist-mounted 7.62mm Gatling guns (also called miniguns) to hose down the open area below the battery. The heavy shooting lasted most of two hours.

The fight turned when an APC clanked slowly up the hill on its steel tracks through the battery positions and right up and over some of the last VC sappers. The big pig stopped, backed up, and clanked over them again. Sporadic firing continued all night as the last few sappers were found and dug out by hand.

John and I stayed hunkered down until first light. Just as we stood up and began to unkink our bodies, firing came from the mess hall behind us. The mess chief was opening the mess hall as Marines were still poking and probing for sappers. He opened one of the pantries and was shot dead by a VC hiding inside. One of the cooks stepped forward and shot the sapper several times through the pantry door, then the VC's body was dragged outside and one of the cooks, in a rage, emptied an M-16 magazine into it.

It would be another four months before Jimi Hendrix would play his guitar rendition of the national anthem at Woodstock. Two years later, when I first heard the recording, I thought it surely must be blasphemous. But I was still quite uptight about my patriotism back then. Now, if they ever make this into a movie, this would be the place for Jimi to play his song.

The morning sun revealed smoke curling up from multiple locations around the hill as the first choppers arrived to get the wounded out. The battery had taken the brunt of the fighting and the casualties. We had ten dead Marines and seventy-five dead VC. We all considered it a big victory.

The battalion surgeon had spent the first thirty minutes of the fight hugging the floor of the officers' four-holer. First, the generator was torched right next to him, and then the plywood around him kept being perforated by bullets from both sides as the battle moved back and forth. "I was afraid the guy with the flamethrower would try to hide in there with me," he said in his lilting Caribbean voice.

At midmorning I went to the dispensary to check on the doctor. We had gotten all the wounded Marines out early, and now the local civilians with wounds and complaints were getting their turn. The doctor called me over to an old mamma-san sitting on a bench. He gently turned her head and tilted it sideways.

"Look at this," he said as he held my finger to the side of her head. About two inches above her ear there was a quarter inch of a flechette dart sticking out. On the opposite side of her head he had found a small black "plus" mark where the dart had entered. "You can almost hang your hat on it," he said. "It has passed right through her brain, but she is cognizant and otherwise fit." I asked what he would do for her and he said, "All we do here is stabilize. She will go to Da Nang and they can worry about it." The old lady gave us her best betel nut smile.

That afternoon I hatched a plan to take up a collection and go to Da Nang for party supplies. Our FAC captain bought into the idea with enthusiasm, and I changed from my dirty camouflage utilities into my cleanest green ones. When the 1600 chopper left for the bright lights, I was aboard. I had Frank Ehrle's office number clutched in my hand when we landed, and he was happy to hear from me. In twenty minutes he had a jeep there to pick me up, and the first thing he had me do when I arrived at his quarters was take another shower.

"You smell like the bush," he said almost apologetically. He pointed to my green utilities and said to the sailor standing by, "Burn these and get the lieutenant some camos." He explained that only Marines wore the plain green utilities anymore, and that the navy would not allow Marine officers into some places. Even after I had bathed and changed, he still thought I smelled "bushy." "We'll go to the Stone Elephant tonight. It is all navy now. If they find out you're a Marine, they won't let you in." The navy seemed to have a lot on its mind in Da Nang, but it did not appear to me as though much of it had to do with the war.

He took me to the commissary after dinner and I bought wine until I ran out of money. Then we went to the Stone Elephant. The place was originally a restaurant, but by then it had been turned into a club for navy officers. They really did have someone at the door screening out Marines.

The Stone Elephant was jam-packed with cleanly shaven faces and smartly ironed camouflage utilities. The music was incredibly loud, and the smoke hung from the high ceiling down to below your shoulders. If you actually wanted to breathe, you had to sit down. We had a great time.

The next morning Frank sent me to the back door of a navy mess hall with my story about being overrun at Liberty Bridge. The mess chief instantly came up with twenty-five or thirty pounds of lobster tails. They gave me an old boxy briefcase filled with ice and lobster, and I boarded the morning chopper back to the bridge with water streaming out of my carry-on luggage and bottle necks sticking out of my new camo blouse. Back at the country club that night, the staff NCOs and officers had a steak-and-lobster mess.

Life on the bridge was a good example of the saying "War is 90 percent boredom and 10 percent stark terror." With the big fight and mess night behind us, it took only a few days of routine for John and me to find ourselves solidly back into the other 90 percent.

The hottest part of the day was from 1500 until 1700. If the breeze failed, it could be miserable.

We were up in our donut only a few days later with a fully loaded A-6 on the horn. We were looking through the ship's glass, plotting out an azimuth and computing meters into feet. I don't know who saw him first, but suddenly we had a live target.

Four thousand meters east of us and one thousand meters from the southern vegetation line was a black pajama in a cone hat. He had a water buffalo with him and it appeared he was working, or perhaps plowing, around the edge of a large bomb crater. I never knew the details for the rules of engagement in our free-fire zone. I don't think we'd ever really had a live target before. In any event, this would give us a real target to shoot at and maybe take our minds off the heat for a while.

This guy was trespassing in our free-fire zone, and the punishment for him would be death by 500-pound bomb. We had already given the pilot his first drop point when we spotted our transgressor. We would wait for the bomb to hit, then make a correction back toward the farmer. Half a minute later we heard, "Bombs away." Depending on altitude, it takes about ten seconds for the bomb to fall. It detonated one thousand meters short but close to being on line with the target. The cone hat did not even look up.

Now it would take three to four minutes for the correction to be calculated and for the plane to line up for another drop. We gave a long correction on a better line in order to get a clear bracket without alarming our target.

The casualty radius for a 500-pound bomb is five hundred meters. If you drop a stick of twenty-four bombs fifty meters apart, you should get pretty good coverage of an area more than one thousand meters long and five hundred meters wide. We centered the stick between the two marking bombs. With any luck, we might get one of the bombs into the crater right next to him.

The bracket bomb was perfect. It was on line and one thousand meters beyond our target. But as we were ready to give the final correction to the pilot, the farmer stood up and looked at the bracket bomb. Then he slowly turned and looked behind him in the direction of the first marking bomb. He stood for a moment and then looked back at the bracket bomb. He was not stupid.

Suddenly he and the water buffalo turned and started to run south as hard as they could run. They were headed across one thousand meters of free-fire zone.

"Uh oh," said John as he peered through the glass. "There he goes. He must be headed for the tree line and the village." The village was five or six deserted huts at the edge of a long tree line.

We quickly recalculated azimuth and a new distance. We called the aircraft and gave them the new data, and told them to drop the load in one stick. Very shortly the bombardier called back, "This seems like a very big correction from the first two drops. It's not even on line. You sure this is correct?" We had originally given the crew "enemy bunkers" as the target designation, so if the crew was paying attention, this was a natural question.

Regardless of the rules of engagement, we suddenly felt like covering our butts. "Roger that," we called back. "We have spotted a VC squad in the open, with weapons."

The farmer was running with a staff; that makes a weapon. And we assumed that the water buffalo was communist.

The flight crew called back, almost begging to go on a visual drop. They had the enthusiasm of someone who never gets to see his own work. "We can find them visually. I know we can . . . come on, let us get them." But I did not want one of Uncle's A-6s swooping down out of the sky onto a lone cone hat and a water buffalo. It took us a moment to argue the crew out of it. Finally they lined up on the target and began their run.

Through the glass we saw the water buffalo get tired. About five hundred meters out, he slowed to a walk. It would save his life. The cone hat was strong and kept up a fast pace.

Another problem arose. The FAC party leader, our captain, was monitoring the radios, and "VC squad in the open" brought him out of the CP with his binoculars. "What have you got?" he asked.

Obfuscate: To darken or dim. To confuse. (To deceive with facts.)

We responded, "We have at least two . . . or maybe three VC." Vaguely, "There may be a couple more, but I think maybe they just split up." He looked out with his binoculars but saw nothing. "They seem to be headed for that tree line in the far southwest corner. We are dropping a stick on it."

Now the battalion XO was out along with two more staff officers. Another Marine stopped by. The FAC party leader turned to the XO. "We have four or five VC with weapons. They are headed for that tree line. I have an A-6 dropping some 500-pounders on the trees." By this time the cone hat was at the edge of the trees and still going strong. Then the radio crackled with a re-signed and disappointed, "Bombs away."

John stood up from the radio and said, "Gentlemen, I give you twenty-four 500-pound bombs." Several seconds passed, and then the tree line exploded with a long continuous string of flashes and a long giant geyser of dirt and smoke.

We were right on target. It all happened at once, and the trees were temporarily obscured. Someone in the crowd called out, "You got a secondary." Sure enough, there was the distinctive off-center flash of a secondary explosion. It meant that we had hit something.

"All right then!" yelled the XO. "Let's get a reaction squad. Let's get a reaction platoon. We will need a chop-per. . . ." This was not good. If we sent Marines out there and one got hurt. . . . This was not good.

John and I made a routine call for a bird and were told that it was currently 1630. That meant that, except for emergencies, the choppers were all busy on already scheduled runs. We would have to call this an emer-gency in order to get a bird. The options were kicked around the group of us for a minute or two, and we de-cided instead to go eat dinner.

John and I never spoke about it. We put our gear away,

went to eat dinner, played an evening of cards, and, as on each and every day of the war, tried to forget it.

It was late morning the next day before we had our first call. The sun was already beating down hot on the sandbags when I sat down, map in hand, to crank up the process. We had an A-6 about to come on station with a full load of bombs, and we had to have a target. John was at the glass, looking for "enemy bunkers," when he suddenly jerked like he had just been kicked in the pants.

"Willie," he said slowly, looking in my direction with a stupid smile. "You won't fucking believe. . . ."

I stood up wondering what he was talking about and peered through the ship's glass. There, four thousand meters south, was a black pajama with a cone hat and a water buffalo. He appeared to be at the very same bomb crater, trying to finish plowing the row he had been chased from the day before.

John was right. I was absolutely stunned. We really both were. We had just dropped twenty-four 500-pound bombs right on him. I have no idea how that farmer survived, but I was impressed. I saw some really bad shooting in Vietnam, too, and much of it was my own.

Two things happened right then, like the snap of our fingers. First, I was surprised by how relieved John and I both were; we were pleased and relieved to see the farmer alive and apparently perfectly fit. Second, and more profound, for the first time, the futility of our effort hit me hard in the face, that we *could not* win this war. We might not lose it, but no matter how long we stayed there, no matter how much firepower we had, we could not win by doing what we were doing.

Hindsight is always more clear, but I had always believed, assumed, that we would win. Even though we were on the verge of withdrawal, I believed that our cause was just, and I had never doubted that somehow we would win.

We dropped the A-6's load of bombs that morning well out of the way, and the farmer paid it no attention. But there was a flash of doubt that I did not want. John and I still had six months of war in front of us. I pushed it out of my consciousness, to the very back of my mind. "If I survive and rotate, then someday I will sit down and think about all this." But not today. No doubts today.

5

In the Summer of '69: Retribution

What goes up
Must come down
Spinning wheel's
Got to go around. . . .

Someone's waiting
Just for you
Spinning wheel,
Spinning true
Drop all your troubles by the riverside
Ride a painted pony
Let the spinning wheel fly.
—BLOOD, SWEAT AND TEARS, "Spinning Wheel"

Payback is a motherfucker.
—OLD MARINE CORPS SAYING

It was the first week of May 1969. Back in the World, American taxpayers had just finished sending in all their tax dollars to Uncle. Over in "the Nam," 5th Marines headquarters was busy thinking up ways to spend some of those dollars. Periodically, when the brass at An Hoa got tired of the pounding they were taking from all the incoming, they sent a battalion or more across the river and into the valley and foothills to the west.

John and I were told to draw any gear we would need to stay out for two weeks. He would be attached to

Charlie Company, and I would go with Bravo; 1/5 was going to move. "Fuck this waiting around, let's go pick a fight."

If you were going out for a few days, it was suitable to use a standard Marine Corps–issue backpack. But you could not carry much gear in the standard pack of the day. If you were going to be out for a while and you wanted an air mattress and some other creature comforts, you found yourself an NVA pack. Those packs would carry almost twice as much gear as a standard-issue Marine Corps pack, and that was more than I intended to carry. Battalion supply had everything we needed, including captured NVA packs and more. At high noon the next day, John and I saddled up and crossed the bridge to the rendezvous point. We were as ready as we could be. "Didn't we already finish this part of our tour?"

As we discovered, we were not the only Marines in 1/5 reluctant to go. The story flashed through camp that one young Marine had placed his hand on a rail of the bridge and had a friend smash it with a two-by-four. When no bones broke, he put the hand up and had it smashed again. When no bones broke the second time, he wrapped the hand in a towel and went to get his pack.

The plan was for battalion HQ and three companies (a battalion minus) to move from Liberty Bridge and sweep the valley to the west and north of An Hoa. The old-timers called the area Arizona Territory. The terrain was mostly open and rolling, with large areas of mostly deserted paddies. Otherwise it was just lots of rock and gravel, almost no shade. Farther west, the valley narrowed and the mountains on each side climbed to thirty-five hundred feet. Foothills ran along the edges of the valley and around the far west end, where the valley narrowed down to make a kind of rounded V into the hill country. Beyond that, the real mountains began. Our operation would stay on the valley floor and in the foothills.

The plan was to operate with two companies maneuvering through the valley and one company back with the battalion CP. The headquarters unit would do some moving around, but would act primarily as a blocking force on the west side of the river, across from An Hoa. Bravo and Charlie companies would be the maneuver companies. If we couldn't stop the bombardment of incoming enemy rounds, at least we might spoil their aim.

Aside from the three weeks I did on Hill 52, most of my experience had been on short patrols that lasted twenty-four hours or less. I located Bravo's CP just off the east end of the bridge. As I dropped my gear next to the radios, the thought crossed my mind that staying out for an extended period and maneuvering in the field with an entire line company would be a new experience.

If I had known then that it would be eighty days before I ate my next cooked meal, I would have given my breakfast that morning the respect it deserved.

I had been assigned two radiomen for some reason. In Vietnam, the job of radio operator was often a reward for surviving six months walking point. That would describe these two Marines. They both looked at carrying a radio as a step back from death. Not that a radio antenna whipping around in the air couldn't draw a lot of fire.

I once asked two carrier pilots, "What was the scariest part of a bombing raid into North Vietnam?" They both answered without hesitation, "Landing on a carrier at night." They both agreed that "sometimes it doesn't matter how good you are."

You could say the same about walking point. Some Marines became very good at it. And some of them liked doing it. But sometimes it didn't matter how good you were.

The two young Marines filled me in on Bravo Company. The CO was Capt. Gene Castagnetti. He had a reputation for being the best company commander in the battalion. He was very good and very bright. The captain was on his second tour. He had collected a handful of medals from his first tour as a platoon commander and, as it would turn out, he would win himself another handful of medals before the coming eighty days had passed. I did not know it at the time, but on his first tour he was an adviser to the ARVN (Army of the Republic of Vietnam, or South Vietnamese troops) in this same Arizona Territory. Knowing he would be going there again, he had been drilling Bravo on the skills his troops would need. Captain Castagnetti's preparation would pay off for us in a big way. It would also keep many more Marines alive.

The gunnery sergeant for Bravo Company was a real horse. Gunny Don Henderson was six feet four inches tall and weighed 240 pounds. His arms were as big as my legs, and his shaved bald head was shiny black; he looked like a shiny black Mr. Clean. While he was not known to yell very often, there was no question that he was ready to enforce the rules.

Uniform of the day would be boots with no socks, trousers with no shorts, and green T-shirt. I had my cartridge belt on suspenders. On top was my flak jacket with binoculars slung across. Last was my helmet and, around my neck, the ever-present green towel. You rolled your trouser legs up to midcalf during the day, you rolled them down and drew the drawstrings tight at night. And don't forget the pack.

Why no socks or underwear? We would be wet almost every day and sometimes all day. My boots, trousers, and virtually all my other gear would dry out quickly anytime they had a chance. But underwear and especially socks don't ever dry out. The first time your boots are soaked, if you remove your socks, put your boots back on, and let the boots dry on your feet, the boots will fit you, literally, like a glove. After a week, I could count my toes without taking my boots off. To spend time drying out your socks and shorts in combat conditions was considered too fastidious.

Human skin is a marvelous material, but it's mostly water. If skin stays wet for seventy-two hours, it will begin to decompose. In 1995 an American pilot flying for NATO was shot down over Bosnia. He hid and survived for six days due to his training, his wits, and his courage. When he was rescued, his only physical problem was that his feet had developed a case of rot from staying wet too long. If he had ditched his socks the first time his boots became soaked, he could have saved himself that trouble, too.

I was not eager to go outside the wire and fight the war close up again. One good bit of news was that there would be no mines. Arizona was no-man's-land. Both sides constantly moved large numbers of new troops through it. If anyone planted mines there, it would jeopardize his own troops, so no one did.

If I had to go out, this was the way for me. I would

have a Marine Corps rifle company around me, and I would carry hell's fire in my right hand (my radio handset). I had supreme confidence in my ability to provide all the air support Bravo Company would need. The enemy would want to kill me with the first shot. Once I got to ground and got my radio working, anyone who shot at us would have to answer to the Wing. I might not be the meanest mother in the valley, but along with John and our FAC party leader, I would be one of the three meanest.

It was late afternoon before we moved out. For the first three days we moved only at night and lay low in the daytime. The enemy had a large number of mortars hidden in the valley and in the foothills. We would be moving around and among them. The company commander had to constantly weigh the value of sitting down to rest against the danger of being located by an enemy FO and getting mortared.

At night the company moved in a long single-file column to keep from getting separated. In the daytime, with no shade to be found, we stretched our poncho liners between the limbs of the brush to create some shade. You had to crawl or crouch to get underneath, but it was worth it. Living outdoors for a couple of months can give one a whole new appreciation for something as simple as shade.

When we had moved westward far enough to be due north of An Hoa, we fanned out. We also began moving during the daytime. We maintained radio contact with Charlie and Battalion, but in order to broaden our search, the three units remained widely separated for the most part. At times we received intelligence from Battal-

ion and an occasional request to go to a certain area, but
we did most of the hunting on our own.

The CO for Bravo Company was good, and he had us
trying hard. He might move us all day for two or three
days, then sit for a day, then move all night one night,
hunker low for a day, and move all night again, hoping
to pop up unexpectedly. We spread out and swept, but
that was slow going. We would move in column to cover
distance.

We knew that the enemy was out there somewhere,
and we tried hard to find him. Arizona was a big place.
We had five hundred Marines fanned out using binoculars and an occasional AO overhead. For the first four
weeks we had almost no contact with the enemy. Nevertheless, with a rifle battalion in the field, armed and
loaded, we had five Marines killed, two of them in
Bravo Company. How does it happen?

It is close to midnight. Bravo is moving west along a
low hogback ridge called the Hot Dog. We are on the
north side, strung along a low dike in a long single column headed west. I'm in the middle of the line, trying to
keep my footing in the darkness.

Suddenly toward the front of the column, M-16 fire
begins to the right front. In the confusion, Marines drop
flat on both sides of the dike. Most of us drop on the left
side, but about a quarter of the column dives to the
right.

Now, Marines up and down the line begin firing to
the right flank. They have no targets; it is just poor fire
discipline. All the Marines on the right side scramble to
jump left. It is pitch black, and as one Marine on the
right side rises to his knees, he is shot, point-blank, in

the chest. He is about five men back from me. I hear someone say, "He's dead." The firing peters out and the night grows quiet. The word whispers up the line to the CO, "We have a casualty." Everyone stands pat, and in just seconds the CO and gunny stride out of the darkness.

We have to take the dead Marine with us. You cannot call for a routine chopper at night, and we have someplace else to be at sunup. The gunny and the squad leader walk off into the darkness to the left and come back after a few minutes with a freshly cut six-foot pole. We tie the dead Marine's hands and feet and sling him under the pole like a game animal. For the next five hours, three Marines trade off on one end of the pole and the gunny carries the other end. The gunny is a horse.

A few days later, a squad of ten Marines is moving up a hill to higher terrain. It has rained off and on all morning.

Just after first light there is a report of NVA to our west, but now it is late morning and we have found nothing. The ground is sloppy and the slope is steep; you have to watch your step to keep from slipping down. In the brush to the right, something snaps loudly. Everyone goes down, safeties off. For two full minutes no one moves.

Eyes search the foliage for a shape or a movement. Nothing. The point man stands up, turns, and slowly starts up the hill again. Now everyone gets up and starts to move up the hill. Suddenly a Marine slips. He falls forward on his knee and elbow. The butt of his M-16 strikes the ground and the weapon fires. The Marine in front of him groans and falls forward. In seconds he is dead. It happens so quickly and so irrevocably, and the incident costs more than just one life. A young man has killed his best friend. He will carry this moment with him for the rest of his life.

You must pull the dead man's poncho from his pack. You double it and lay him on it. You grab the four corners and slide back down the hill to a flatter, more open place where a helicopter can land.

To the feelings of grief and anger and frustration, you can add a large dose of guilt. By one count, 40 percent of our casualties in Vietnam were friendly fire. From my experience, that number may be only slightly high. If you add casualties from accidents, helicopters colliding, and the like, and a category for nonhostile casualties, then I can easily believe that a full third of our dead and wounded were caused by us and not the enemy. We took a terrible toll on ourselves. Given the way we fought the war, I suppose it was inevitable.

As I stood on the side of that hill and looked across the valley at a CH-46 whopping its way toward us, the words had not yet coalesced in my mind. Perhaps others present had the words fixed clearly in their consciousness, but in the summer of 1969, to say the words would have been to break the faith. No one in Bravo 1/5 was willing to do that yet. Still, the recognition was heavy in the air among us: This is a waste. We are going to withdraw anyway, and this is all a waste. It gave me a sick feeling, and it wouldn't take much for all that anger, frustration, and guilt to turn into bitterness.

If you want to understand why Vietnam veterans were so angry all through the seventies, this would be a good place to start looking. "We are going to pull out anyway, and this is all a waste."

Although we are having trouble locating the enemy, he has little trouble locating us. It must be the local contingent of the Viet Cong, because someone seems to always know where we are. One day we bed down in late afternoon on a small hillock near ruins of what had been a Buddhist temple. After about an hour, just after 2100, there is a very loud *BANG*.

Everyone rolls over, and I hear safeties clicking off in the darkness. For several long minutes no one moves. I hear two Marine voices whispering, but not well enough to know what they are saying. Off in the darkness I hear a quiet *thump*, as though someone has thrown a baseball or a rock to the ground. Five seconds later, in the same general direction, there is another detonation.

The creeps are lofting large Chi-Com grenades at us from somewhere out in the darkness. I have been told that they cut old inner tubes into strips to make a slingshot. Not designed to really hurt anyone, the grenades are made of C-ration cans and are so poorly put together that most of the cans blow out at one end, creating no shrapnel. They are bigger than normal and very loud in the darkness, but unless one lands in your pack, you are not likely to be hurt. They keep it up at a slow pace of one every ten to fifteen minutes for two or three hours. I learn how to sleep, listening not for the detonations, but for the *thumps*.

There were drugs in Vietnam. The Marine Corps, and Bravo Company, had a zero-tolerance policy. That night, the gunny was making his rounds about midnight. As he approached a fighting hole, he smelled dope in the air. The gunny kept walking and never said a word. When he reached the Marine, who was crouched down in his hole, the gunny kicked the young man full in the face, breaking his jaw. The next morning, we medevacked one new believer to Da Nang for an appointment with an orthodontist. Paperwork was kept to a minimum in the bush.

The next night we were in open country. In the late afternoon we moved about fifteen hundred meters north. An hour or so after dark, we stopped. We didn't dig in, but just lay down in place. At about 2200, an hour later than the night before, a loud electronic squawk sounded from out in the distance—the sound of feedback in a loudspeaker. Everyone turned and listened, somewhat tensely. "What are these screwballs up to now?" seemed to be the number one question.

For a moment the evening air was filled with the sound of silence, and then we heard a woman's voice over a loudspeaker, at a distance. "Marines! We do not want to hurt you! Put down your weapons and come to us." I do not remember the whole message, but they of course knew that we were 5th Marines, and were willing to let bygones be bygones if we would only give up our weapons and change sides.

We all got a quiet chuckle out of it. It was less of a nuisance than having those damned C-ration cans exploding all night. I thought it was really quaint of them to pull out an old psy-ops script from the fifties for us. It was almost endearing. We shot the 105s from An Hoa and tried to at least break their speaker, but at night sound moves around on the air and distances are very difficult to judge.

I heard once that in the Old West, the Apache held out

so long against the U.S. Cavalry because of the way each side used its resources. The story goes that the cavalrymen rode their horses until they dropped. The soldiers then put their saddles on fresher horses and rode off after the Apache. Other Apache followed behind, picking up the abandoned horses, riding them another hundred miles, and then eating them. True or not, it is an apt analogy for the war in Vietnam. The Marine Corps is always short of resources and has a reputation for doing more with less. Still, we had all the supplies we wanted while out in Arizona. Each of the three units was resupplied by helicopter every other day.

It is, of course, difficult to remain clandestine with choppers flying in and out. We didn't care. I, for one, preferred the fresh water and adequate supplies to the anonymity. We usually took a resupply just at dusk, then moved at dark. We tried to destroy any extra supplies; we punctured extra C-ration cans and cut up batteries, and then buried the waste. Nevertheless, I am certain that an NVA squad or even a platoon could make a day's ration out of a Marine company's trash. Think for a moment: What do you do with the trash from 190 people every day?

I must say something here about C rations. I think we did conclusively prove after almost three months that you cannot die from eating C rations. You may go crazy, and I do mean rock-throwing berserk, but you cannot die from it. In only a few days your metabolism and body rhythm noticeably slow down. I went from eating three hot meals a day with no exercise at Liberty Bridge to two canned meats, a bread, three cans of fruit, and the condiments of two meals each and every day. In addition, I was getting plenty of exercise. As a result, my weight dropped. I don't know where my weight began or where it ended, but I was soon cinching up a pair of size thirty-two trousers. By the time I got out of Arizona, my morale could no longer transcend the food.

There are different levels of physical conditioning. There is such a thing as being in good shape, and then there is such a thing as "bush shape." If you can hump sixty pounds of gear all day long, sleep on the ground at night, and eat very little from small green cans for five or six weeks, then you are in bush shape. It is a different way to live, and it is not a state of grace. I thought it was miserable, but I was too busy and too scared at the time to complain. Once in a while I had to remind myself, "It's only thirteen months."

Each Sunday everybody took a malaria tablet. I was told it was quinine. I don't know what it was, but it worked. Every corpsman spent a part of every Sunday distributing the pills to his flock.

On the second Sunday out, I pulled an unthinking stunt that almost took me out of the war.

Except for the malaria pill, Sunday was like every other day in the bush. I was already bored with the food, and I did not eat that morning because we were staying in one place and I was not hungry. The corpsman passed out the malaria pills around noon. I took my pill and chased it with most of a quart of apple juice. An hour later I ate a meal, but the damage was already done, and the result was devastating. That night I had diarrhea. The next morning I am sure I ate something, but we moved early and we moved all day.

I spent the morning falling out of line, dropping my pack, pulling my E-tool, doing my business, covering it, and getting myself back together and hustling to catch up with my place. I was worn out by noon. In the afternoon I walked with my E-tool in my hand. I kept drinking water to avoid dehydration. That night I tried to eat, but by that time I was getting pretty miserable.

Tuesday morning I lost complete control of my bowels. When I walked, effluent drained from my body cavity and ran down my legs into my boots. When we stopped, the drainage stopped and it dried. When we moved again, the mess on my legs pulled painfully loose and the drainage began again. I no longer fell out of line; I simply slopped along. I could not eat and was trying to conserve my strength. At noon I finally talked to the corpsman and he gave me a bottle of Pepto-Bismol. I drank that all afternoon, but nothing changed.

That Tuesday night still stands in my mind as the worst night I can ever remember for sheer human discomfort and desperation. A Marine rifle company, in combat, is a macho place to be. It is not a place you drop out of because your tummy is feeling bad. Still, I was in sorry shape. The Marines around me knew I was in trouble, and they left me alone. I wasn't going to shoot myself, but if someone had offered to help me that night, I may have had them do it.

We pulled out early the next morning and I was wobbling. The corpsman had given me another half bottle of the pink miracle, and I felt that I could probably keep up, but I was not sure what might happen if we got into a fight. Luckily, there was no fight, and in the afternoon I was still stumbling along when word came to pull up. The CO said we would stay put until the next night. That was good news for me.

Even better news: The drainage stopped during the morning, almost without my knowing it. I made some shade. My corpsman gave me a salve. I used most of my drinking water to wash my feet and legs. The insides of my legs were red and sore, with several raw spots beginning. I applied the salve and changed trousers. My appetite returned, and I ate everything I could find. By Thursday afternoon my strength began to return, and I knew I would be all right. But it was a lesson to remember.

It would be twenty-two years before I could drink apple juice again. For the first ten years I was like a vampire confronting garlic: my whole body would recoil from even the sight of apple juice at the breakfast table.

You became very tired and very dirty through all this. On the seventeenth day we found a unique spot and stopped for a break to bathe and cool off. I was feeling better, but I was smelling bad; I guess we all were. The local joke was that you know it's time to bathe when the flies start leaving you alone.

We had turned our sweep back to the east, and the company was spread out on two sides of a long draw. We came off a flat shelf and went down to the river bottom. There, in front of the company CP, was a brilliant white beach of white pea gravel. It must have been 50 or 60 meters across to the river and 150 meters long. The river itself was 40 feet across, 4 feet deep, and beautifully, wonderfully clear and cold. Straight out of the mountains, the water tasted sweet.

Vietnam is beautiful. The scene was almost breathtaking. The CO called an immediate halt and the platoons took turns watching, washing, and relaxing. It was a big morale boost for me. While we were laying out, drying, someone called out "Freedom bird!" We all looked up. At thirty-five thousand feet and no doubt serving cocktails, an airliner was heading west. Someone else said, "Headed for Bangkok."

At times like this the conversation can get inane. "What are you going to do when you get home?" one Marine asks.

"Me? I'm going to shoot me a hippie. Do you know why? Because while we are over here getting our asses shot at, those hippies are back in the World, laying in the grass, smoking our dope, and fucking our women. What are you going to do?"

"Me? When I get back to the World, I'm going to lay in the grass, smoke your dope, and fuck your women." Big laugh.

One of the newer Marines starts to tell his story. "I had this good buddy in boot camp . . ." Two or three older Marines almost squeal at once, "*Good buddy?*"

The young man stopped and looked around. "What's wrong?"

One of the snipers said with a smirk, "Don't they teach you assholes anything in boot camp anymore? In the Crotch [the Corps], a good buddy is a guy who will go into town and get two blow jobs, then come back and give you one." There is some snickering.

The young Marine looked at the group for a moment and said, "Oh hell, I knew that. You guys are sick." And I can truly attest to you that we were. Homesick, sick of the killing, sick of the war, sick of it all. But he began his story again, "I knew this dude in boot camp . . ."

I do not remember really bathing again the rest of the way. And I do not remember smelling bad. I am sure I did; I just no longer noticed it.

Two more lessons from Vietnam. When out for extended periods, take care of your feet and your teeth.

When on reduced rations, be careful what you ingest and how you do it.

We ended up on the north side of the valley, headed west. Charlie Company was on the south side moving parallel, as we watched the valley floor from both sides. For several nights in a row we called up F-4s in late afternoon and early evening. We shot the 105s from An Hoa and coordinated enough with the guns to enable them to time an illumination round for ground burst. With a little extra effort we could time the F-4s to begin their roll-in on a napalm run just after we had a shot from the 105s in An Hoa.

The idea was to have the artillery flare ignite just above the ground, and have the jet immediately drop a napalm bomb right on top of it. If everything worked just right, the resulting fire would last for several hours and give us a known grid from which we could adjust artillery fire after dark. It also gave us a visible way for air support to find us in the darkness.

The early result was an illumination round burning on the ground while the jets dropped napalm around it. The next time we tried, we had an illumination round light on the ground, and five seconds later disappear in a wall of flaming jell. On the third night, we got a confirmed kill. The illumination round popped about fifteen feet off the ground and, in the bright glare, someone in pajamas stood up to run. He made about ten steps when he and the illumination round disappeared in the napalm. From far up the line a Marine yells, "Crispy critters!"

The pilot called to us, excitedly, "I saw him! Did you see him? Did I get him?"

We called the pilot back. "Oh, yeah, you got him." It was a lucky target, but damned good shooting. We even called the guns in An Hoa and gave them an "assist." They were delighted. It was a nice evening to be out, and we were all feeling good.

By now we had been out almost four weeks and experienced only scattered contact. That was about to change abruptly. Beginning at the end of May, one of our three units would be in contact every day for the next nine or ten days in a row. Some of the contact was brief or fleeting, but a good deal of it would be heavy.

High noon. The company is strung out in a long column, pushing through tree lines and across paddies, daring anyone to shoot at us. Up ahead, two M-16s fire to the right front. Now the column is running forward, trying to get through the next tree line, hoping to get some action. There is no return fire. When I break out of the trees I see five khaki uniforms beating feet. By now they are two hundred meters out and headed east. I step to the side and stop. Twenty-plus M-16s are firing at the receding enemy, with no effect. Marines keep extending the firing line; everyone is standing and firing offhand. In a moment there are perhaps fifty grunts standing in a giant firing line, pumping lead, much of it going who-knows-where.

When I had been with Mike Company, the troops there had displayed poor fire discipline at times. Now Bravo Company was showing that poor fire discipline was endemic to most rifle companies in Vietnam. There were good examples, of course, but there were many more bad examples.

It drove the NCOs crazy. I must admit, at times it just felt good, safer, to rip off a few rounds. But poor fire discipline is the sign of an amateur. The enemy usually had excellent fire discipline. At times we did, too, but generally we did not. It was my biggest criticism of our effort. And of course, these enemy soldiers escaped.

The addiction of war was in us. As tired and as bored as you become when fighting fatigue and the heat, all it takes is a shout or someone moving too fast and suddenly you have never felt so alert, so alive. Your nose, your ears, your eyes, all working suddenly better than ever before. It is a real rush.

The days and the fights run together in my memory. You simply do what you must at the time, and then go on to the next problem. There are, however, a few moments so vivid that they stand out, even after all these years. Like this fight—I don't even remember how it began.

The company is spread out, moving basically west. I hear shooting up front. Now everyone is moving forward at a faster pace. Suddenly to my immediate left an enemy machine gun opens fire directly at us.

I drop behind a log with two or three others. Marines scramble behind a low berm, and in fifteen seconds a dozen or more of us are pinned down tight. The machine gun is very close, perhaps only fifty feet away. We must have walked up behind him, because the tangle of brush and vegetation is so thick that he has no field of fire. Maybe this is why no one is hit. I don't know how much ammunition he has, but as he continues hammering away, he is clearing himself a field. Some rounds are snapping straight through, and some are glancing around. He is so close that when the wind shifts our way, I can smell his smoke. We are in deep trouble.

An AO in an OV-10 Bronco spotter plane checks in. I call him up and describe our emergency. We lay out air panels at both ends of our line, and so does the next closest unit.

The pilot quickly identifies us and the enemy gunner. The Bronco rolls in and fires his 7.62mm Gatling gun. I am sure it can be effective, but it sounds thin and reedy firing all by itself. Either the brush is too thick or the gunner has good cover, because the strafing run has no effect. The Bronco makes a tight turn and runs in again, this time with 2.75-inch rockets. Again there is no effect.

The AO has a pair of F-4s on station with napalm and 250-pound bombs. The bombs are out of the question; we are much too close to the target. He tells us he will have the jets drop their napalm. I am concerned that we are still too close—fifty feet—for napalm. I do not want any napalm in my lap. The AO calls back and advises us to pull out our ponchos and cover ourselves, just in case.

I give him a quick check fire. "If it's that tight," I tell him, "I don't want it." Still, we must have some relief. Very soon we will start taking casualties.

"In that case," he says, "how about the twenty Mike Mike [20mm cannon]?" It sounds much more precise than the splashy old napalm. "Okay," I say. "Hurry."

I am lying flat in the dirt, leafing back through the dusty pages of my mental notebook to a Saturday morning almost a year earlier in the Chocolate Mountains of California. Our class of would-be FACs was standing on the side of the mountain watching the jets "nape" and strafe some dummy targets about a mile away down on the valley floor.

If my numbers are correct, from approximately a half mile away and traveling at 450 knots, the pilot will loose a three-second burst from his Gatling gun that will fire perhaps two hundred 20mm cannon rounds, with exploding heads, into an area about half the size of a football field, which must be 75 by 150 feet. We have to have some relief, but this still sounds very tight.

A jet fighter does not turn a corner like a car. When the pilot wants to turn, he stands the airplane up on its left wing and pulls back on the stick. Down on the ground, from the target's perspective, the plane makes a wide sweeping skid with its belly pushing flat against the air. When the pilot has the nose pointed in the target's direction, he lays the wings down flat again and begins to kick the rudders left and right to line up the sights.

The nose of the fighter swings from left of the target, across the target, across me, and out to my right. Then back across me, across the target, and out to the left. Then back toward me, wing up, wing down. As it cuts through the air, the jet almost looks like a toy.

I can see him correct his slope as he raises and lowers the nose, which is now pointed directly at me. My whole body begins to crawl with fear. "My God, what have I done? I've killed us all!"

The first sign I have that the fighter aircraft is firing its Gatling gun is a thin stream of black smoke trailing the aircraft. The next signal is the ground to my left exploding in a long, loud, rolling roar. The ground under my body shakes so violently that dust rises several inches into the air; I have the sensation that the air is being sucked from my lungs. Struggling to catch my breath, I manage to inhale dirt up my nose and into my mouth. Then there is silence.

I am trying to make enough spit to call for a check fire, when I look up and see the second F-4, already out of his turn and kicking his rudders from my right, across me, across the target, and out to the left. Then, back across, toward me again. Wing up, wing down. The second-best pilot up there is about to test his skill.

I see the telltale black smoke trailing the aircraft. I take a breath, close my eyes, and hug the earth. The long, loud, rolling roar begins. The earth is shaking so hard I cannot believe it. The dust rises off the ground. The longest three seconds in mankind's recorded history ends. There is silence.

I key the handset and almost yell, "Check fire, Cowpoke! No more. I give you one confirmed and an automatic weapon."

The Bronco pilot calls back something cute like, "Call us anytime, Laundry Man. We aim to please."

Up and down the line the men are coughing. Someone shouts "Yeowie, shit!" Someone else shouts, "Is that it?"

"Yes, that's it," I call out. "No more." Someone pokes his head up. Fires a shot, then fires another shot.

"Good shooting, Lieutenant. I think you got him." A big laugh as Marines scramble to their feet and hustle off to find the fight.

All but one, perhaps; I stick my head up. Where before there had been heavy vegetation standing six feet or higher, there is now a dirty gray pall of dust and smoke hanging three or four feet off the ground. Nothing else.

I get up, one leg at a time. My whole insides are still quaking. My legs are noticeably weak. Am I the only one to just have the bejeezus scared out of him? I think for a moment about what it means to be alive, but catch myself quickly and shove the thought to the back of my mind. If I survive and rotate, then someday I will sit down and think about all this. But not today. It is too dangerous to think today. Just do your job and keep up. And try not to kill yourself!

The Marine Corps is the best in the world at close, co-ordinated supporting fires. This one should go somewhere in that log. O ye of little faith, Semper Fi.

June 7, 1969. We had played chase-and-duck with a much more aggressive enemy for two days. Bravo had worked its way to the far west end of the valley. We were up in the foothills on the north side, still moving west. The 105s at Liberty Bridge were out of range, but that did not worry me; we still had the 155s, the 8-inch, and the Wing.

It had been raining off and on for three days, and pouring down hard much of the morning. One platoon had split off from the company the night before; it was located about two thousand meters south, across the valley floor, in the foothills on the south side. We had two platoons and the CP strung out in a long column with flank security hacking through semiheavy brush.

The CO called for a halt at about noon. It was too wet to eat, and before I could even think about a good place to sit down, the CO called a staff meeting. When we gathered together, he said that Battalion had called. As we all knew, many NVA were moving in the area. Battalion said that the enemy may be planning to mass and that we should get the company back together and prepare to move back east to support the rest of the battalion.

Also, An Hoa had reported taking incoming rockets at about the same time our forward observer, Lt. Chuck

Bolish, had reported seeing flashes in the foothills to our south.

The CO then said that one platoon, with the gunny, would detach now and move south directly across the valley to link up with the platoon already there. The third platoon would also leave now and follow a small arc the captain had drawn on his map. It went across a hill about one thousand meters to our west and south and then back east to join up with the other two platoons. He then drew another arc on the map. It went southwest more than one thousand meters behind two hills, out to the edge of the map page. It then turned back east, across the river and several hills, and finally southeast again to join with the rest of the company. He said that the company CP along with the two snipers, a machine gun, and two more riflemen to walk point and drag (last man), would wait thirty minutes and follow that route to do a little reconnaissance.

I could not believe what I was hearing. He was going to send 150 rifles on direct routes to some rendezvous point. Then he would take fourteen of us, with four radios and a bunch of pistols, farther out and away—into an extremely dangerous situation.

It gets worse. Because of the rain and dense low clouds, we could not shoot artillery and no one could fly. Artillery rounds, even armed with delay fuses, will detonate in dense clouds. And with visibility almost zero, there would be no AO and no air strikes.

As soon as the meeting broke up, both the gunny and I were standing tall, right in front of Castagnetti.

"Are you sure this is a good idea, Skipper? We can't fly and we can't shoot. If we get caught out there, we will have to eat these radios," was my concern.

"Sir, you ought to take a platoon or at least two squads," chipped in the gunny.

"No. It'll be okay," he said. He was fiddling with his map and his compass, and never looked directly at either of us. "We aren't going far. I just want to look, that's all."

As I walked away, I thought, "I volunteered for this, so mine is not to reason why, but is this necessary? The rest of us are not lifers. The rest of us would like to go home." If we got caught out there, no one would know for hours and no one could even look for us. We would simply disappear.

I had grown to respect the CO. He was as sharp as his reputation and he always stayed one step ahead. I would rather be with him, even doing something crazy, than not. But now I was beginning to worry. We waited thirty minutes, and then sometime before 1300 the fourteen of us headed off to the west. The sky opened up again and it began pouring down rain as hard as any we had seen in three days. We immediately started down a steep, muddy grade that had us skidding part-time on the seat of our pants. When we got down off the hill, we turned southwest and headed back up again. It rained so hard at times that I could barely make out the Marine in front of me.

In boot camp, the DIs (drill instructors) had us do a devilish drill called "hooking up." Each Marine carries an E-tool strapped to the back of his pack. On the command "Hook up," everyone steps forward and grabs the handle of the E-tool in front of him. The DIs do it for punishment. Immediately, every link in the chain begins to jerk against every other link. If you happen to have any juice left in your legs when you start, this is guaranteed to drain it. We had to link up twice that day just to keep from separating. I began to worry less about getting in a fight than about being washed away and drowning.

Before we started, I had guessed that it would take us three or four hours to make our loop and find our way back to the company. I had not looked at my watch since we started, and in the rain and slop I lost track of time. I had my compass in my hand, but I had not looked at it. It seemed that we had been going for a long time. We were to cross a trail on the second hill and turn back east.

I was fourth from the back of the column. I had my head down, trying to keep my balance and wondering when we would find our turn, when I ran into the Marine in front of me. The column had stopped. The rain was lighter and I could see the CO and the FO looking at their maps, comparing ideas. I made my way to the front of the column in time to hear the CO say, "So, we might be here, but then, that's not right."

We had missed our turn. As the three of us looked at the maps and turned round and round, we could not find anything to match what we could see on the ground. It appeared, much as I did not want it to appear, that we had not only missed our turn, we had walked off the edge of the map page and were not able to locate ourselves with our current gear. This was becoming worse and worse.

What to do? We did not know how far south we had gone, and the ridges were running north and south, so heading due east was not the best option. We turned back to the north and rolled over the ridges eastward when we could. It was easy to miss the turn on those old maps, but now we were in trouble. The rain eased at times, but the clouds were still too heavy to shoot artillery.

If the sky lightened up, we could shoot the 155s at a known spot and locate ourselves. But if the weather stayed like this, not only would there be no supporting fires, we could not even tell anyone who wanted to help where to look for us.

It is almost an hour since we slogged our way around a hill, down across a small valley, and then north again. We are hoping to recognize a piece of ground or get back to the river. The column is walking along the long axis of a ridge, about halfway up the side. It is rocky, so the water drains well and the walking is easier. I am becoming very tired, and I know the radiomen are dragging butt by now.

Suddenly the CO takes off at a run straight up the hill to our right. It startles me, but others do not even seem to notice. When he gets about twenty-five meters up the hill, he turns around, levels his rifle, and fires three shots over our heads. "Bang, bang, bang! You're all dead! Did you know that? You are all dead!" The column seems to stumble to a halt. Everyone stands for a moment gawking at the skipper. He is standing there now, pumping his fingers at us in mock recoil.

The thought flashes through my mind that I am second in command. If he cracks up, I will have to get the rest of us back. Then I begin to wake up. Others seem to wake up, too. The whole column has been walking along taking a nap. We are up to our butts in trouble, and there can be no resting until we get out. This is the CO's wake-up call, as bizarre as it seems at the time. The captain sends one of the snipers up the ridge another twenty-five meters for flank security. That lasts only about ten minutes, and then the brush gets so thick that he must drop back into the column. But suddenly everyone is awake, and as it turns out, just in time.

The radio operators put fresh batteries into each radio and begin to ditch the rest of their gear to lighten their loads. My pack feels like it weighs a hundred pounds, and the straps are cutting into my shoulders, even through the padding of my flak jacket. The column turns east again and starts up another ridge. It is safer up on top. I am still toward the back of the column and am only halfway to the top when a harsh whisper rolls down the hill, "Machine gun up!"

The first words that come to my mind are, "Oh shit, we're dead." The machine gunner steps out of line, takes one more step, and falls flat on his face. I am next behind him. I jump out and drop on my hands and knees. I get my shoulder up under his rump and start to dig. He catches his traction and shoots up the hill to the top, and I fall flat on my face. I get up, pumping for the top. My heart is in my throat.

As my eyesight clears the top of the ridge, I see an open area about fifty feet across and a hundred feet long. An M-16 opens fire—slow semiautomatic fire— down the other side. *Pop, pop, pop.* Now another M-16 begins, *pop, pop, pop.* All outgoing.

I am not the only Marine who is scared. The CO's radioman is sitting on the ground with his legs splayed out in front of him like a little kid. He is almost crying. "They're everywhere," he whines, "they're everywhere. We're going to die right here. I don't want to die. Not here."

The machine gunner runs across the opening to the other edge, points his M-60 down the slope, and rips off a burst. Immediately the skipper grabs him by the neck, shouting, "Short bursts! Well-aimed shots!"

The corpsman steps up to me and hands me his M-16 and a bandolier of magazines. "Take this, Lieutenant. I'll break out my gear." Now both snipers and the FO are firing that same slow *pop, pop, pop*.

I throw the bandolier over my shoulder and hustle to the left end of the firing line. I step to the edge and look down. Two hundred feet below and about thirty degrees out from my feet, the river is raging from three days of rain. The first thing I see is a khaki uniform in the water on the far side of the river. He is pulling himself out of the river by a tree limb.

I open fire. I hit him four times in the back, and his body sags back into the river. The current grabs him and pulls him away from the trees. I fire until the khaki disappears underwater. But if we are in so much trouble, why are *they* swimming the river?

I look up the firing line to my right. The Marine walking drag has just stepped up and started to fire. To his right is the FO, then the two snipers, then the point man, and last the machine gunner. Burst of three . . . burst of three. The skipper is still holding him with the right hand on the flak jacket, and with his left hand he is pointing at targets or helping lift the M-60's muzzle for the next target. The CO is talking intently in the gunner's ear. The two of them almost look like they are dancing. By now the volume of fire has become strong.

Down at the river, we have trapped a resupply column. When the shooting started, NVA at both ends of the column tried to escape. None of them will make it.

The column has been moving north on a narrow trail next to the river. They have the river raging on their right side and a sixty-degree slope on their left. We start shooting at the front and rear of the column. In the middle, an officer and several of the bearers realize there is no escape. They begin to throw all the weapons, ammunition, and supplies into the water to keep it from capture. They will die in place, doing their jobs.

The CO looks back and sees me. He calls out, "Get on the horn and tell Battalion what we have here." I hurry to the radios.

The skipper's radioman is feeling much better. He almost smiles at me. "We're okay, huh?"

I pick up the battalion handset. "I think so. For now."

I hope that from up on top we can make radio contact. "Latin Rebel, this is Laundry Man. Over."

"Laundry Man, Latin Rebel." It was Battalion, and it was good to hear another voice.

"This is Laundry Man. We have a working alley cat, I say again, we have a working alley cat."

I look up and the CO shouts, "Five!"

I say, "We have five confirmed." Then I remember mine. "We have six confirmed and counting. Over."

"Roger that, Laundry Man. You have a working alley cat with six confirmed and counting. Wait one."

The volume of fire is still going strong. The CO and one of the snipers are starting to take a count. I call Battalion again while I try to keep up with the hand signals and body language.

"Latin Rebel, this is Laundry Man. I have twelve confirmed . . . I have fourteen confirmed . . . I have fifteen confirmed. Over."

The next voice on the radio is the battalion S-3. He is

almost yelling, and in the background someone is yelling. "Roger, Laundry Man!" he says. "You have fifteen confirmed and still counting. What is your current poz [position], Laundry Man?"

I don't know exactly what to say. "This is Laundry Man, we are, um, well, lost, Latin Rebel. We, um, missed a turn . . . I have nineteen confirmed . . . twenty . . . twenty-one confirmed. Over."

When he keys his handset again, there is so much screaming and yelling going on behind him that you would think our bullets are hitting at Battalion instead of down in the gorge. While there is pandemonium going on around him, the S-3's voice takes on a change in tone. He does not seem to know whether to cheer or wring his hands. He is catching on.

The shooting lasted three or four minutes. When it ended, we had twenty-six dead NVA.

The CO took the two riflemen and the two snipers and went down the slope to search the dead. They were looking for either valuable intelligence information or bitching souvenirs. They found some of both. The two riflemen swam the river and searched the five who had managed to cross. At least one NVA soldier was still alive and had to be shot again. Six had died in the water and fifteen had died on our side of the river, either trying to escape or ditching their ordnance. They never seemed to know where we were and they never fired a shot. I wondered if I could have died so bravely.

A dispute flashed briefly between the snipers and the CO. The snipers wanted to mark up some of the dead, to cut "B" in some foreheads. Even better, "It would be powerful medicine," they argued, "to hang a body on a limb by his shirt and cut a large 'Bravo 1/5' on his chest. Let these motherfuckers know who owns this place, anytime we want it."

The CO barely listened. He herded his group back to the top. The NVA would find their dead right where they had fallen. The search group had found a bundle of documents. The skipper carefully wrapped the documents and tucked them away in his pack. One of the riflemen found a beautiful silver-plated 9mm pistol with pearl handles. We also knew that two mortars and a heavy automatic weapon had been ditched into the river, along with enough ammunition to supply a battalion for a day or more. While the CO called back to Battalion, I turned our parade around and got everyone down the hill, headed out.

Actually, we were not in a bad tactical situation. We had fired carefully and had more than half our ammunition left. This dead supply unit would not be missed for hours, and it would be hours more before anyone came looking for them. We could clean up our mess and reset our trap. In a war that mattered, we could hold out here for twenty-four hours, maybe more. We had found our way back to the river, so we could locate ourselves easily. If the weather broke, we could be resupplied and/or reinforced. If it had mattered. But this was Vietnam.

Years later, this day would seem like one of the highlights of my tour, but on the day it happened, it was just more violence, just more killing. I was getting sick of it. I was glad that we were alive, that *I* was alive. But if I had tried to put one word to my feelings at the time, it would have been *flee!* We had our prize; now the trick would be to escape alive.

In about three minutes the CO and his two radios

came sailing past. The column took off with a lurch. I do not remember how we ever did locate ourselves. We continued pushing north and east on a kind of looping route, staying back from the river. It was late afternoon by then. It would be dark soon, and we still had a long way to go.

The adrenaline wore off and exhaustion set in again. No one spoke. No one had to. If I ever doubted whether anyone else was feeling the stress, I only had to look behind me at the faces there.

It was well after dark when we got back to the river. We believed that we were close to the rest of Bravo Company, but crossing the river would be a problem. Word came back to hold hands or hold on to the next man's weapon. The point man had waded halfway out, and the river was chest deep and moving fast. We could cross at this point. The river was eighty feet wide and had a high bank on the other side. I was still third or fourth man from the back of the column. I grabbed a rifle butt behind me and a hand ahead of me. When we went into the water, I had the current to my back.

The point man should have gone all the way across. About twenty feet from the far bank, the old narrow bottom dropped another two feet. The point man swam to the far side and pulled the next Marine across.

Somewhere ahead of me the line broke. Suddenly two Marines were silently floating away. It was pitch black, and they quickly disappeared from sight. We all stopped. It took only a moment for those already across to make a human chain and reach out to us. We each stuck out a rifle barrel and they pulled us across easily. We waited in silence for almost ten minutes for the last two Marines to swim their way to our side of the river and catch up, which they did. We moved only two hundred meters and fired a flare. The company called us back on the radio with a direction from them to the flare, and we shot a back azimuth to get home.

I don't know what time it was when we finally straggled in. I did not talk to anyone or do anything. I dropped my pack and lay down on the side of the hill, in the mud. I removed my binoculars but I kept my flak jacket on.

It started to rain. I felt the rain on my face. I had the sensation that rivulets of water were snaking their way downhill, around and under my body, and then I passed out.

When I awoke the sun was bright. I broke out rations and ate. There was not much talking. We stayed down all day. Late that afternoon we sent the captured documents back to Regiment aboard a resupply chopper. Just at dusk the company moved about two thousand meters east. It was almost midnight, and we fanned out and lay down again, quietly. The CO sent the two snipers and three riflemen out about four hundred meters farther east as a listening post. We all settled in and tried to sleep.

At the listening post, 0230. The younger sniper has the radio watch. Like everyone, he is fighting fatigue. He sits next to the radio with the other four Marines lying around him. His head bobs and then drops to his chest. A moment later he is shaken vigorously by the shoulder. He looks up into the face of an NVA point man. Both young men are so surprised that each fumbles with his weapon before either can respond.

They both fire, point-blank, and both miss. Firing is

immediate from both directions. One Marine sits upright and is shot dead from both sides. The NVA scatter into the nearby brush, and the Marines throw eight or ten hand grenades in behind them. It all lasts less than thirty seconds.

Four hundred meters away, we all sat upright and strained our eyes in the darkness. At night, binoculars act to gather light, and you can see some contrasts. But there was not much to see. The FO was calling in a grid for illumination when the fight petered out and the senior sniper called in. He was talking in a harsh whisper that sounded like coursing adrenaline.

"You heard the fight. They walked right up behind us. There were at least fifteen, maybe a lot more. I've got one dead and one wounded. Over."

The CO called him back. "Where did they go? Can you get back here to us?"

There was no whisper in the sniper's voice this time. "You didn't hear me. I have one dead and one wounded. That leaves three of us to fight. You put me out here, you son-of-a-bitch, you come get me."

In a crouch, I moved over to the CO and volunteered to take a squad to go get the listening post. But the CO seemed embarrassed that he hadn't realized the situation first. He may have been embarrassed that he had been challenged on the company net, with the whole company eavesdropping. In any event, he took a squad out and brought everyone back. The next morning at first light we sent our two casualties to Da Nang, and the next couple of hours passed quietly.

Just after 0900, from the mountains five thousand meters to the north, there was a *boom* followed by the sound of an artillery shell whistling out of the valley. It detonated in a giant geyser of dirt about a thousand meters northeast of us. A moment later my radio crackled to life with John Juracek's voice. "Was that for me, or was that for you?"

Charlie Company was about three thousand meters north and just east of us. After the last few days, it was good to hear John's familiar voice. The round had landed almost evenly between us. I called him back to say hello. He had listened to my conversation with Battalion during the alley cat. "You've been busy," he said. "Are you okay?" I assured him I was fine.

While we were talking, the enemy artillery piece fired again. The round whistled across the valley and right over our heads. It impacted about four hundred meters behind me, but it did not detonate—a dud. John called back. "Congratulations, it's for you."

The ground was rocky and rough. The night before, we had simply lain down where we were. Suddenly the morning air was filled with the *ching, ching, ching* of E-tools striking rock. The enemy shelled us for the next two hours with what must have been an old 75mm left over from the war against the French. The ammunition was old and, knowing our enemy, they may not have even had leveling bubbles on the gun.

They fired about thirty rounds at us that morning, but only half detonated, and they were delay fuse. There was very little shrapnel, but they blew geysers of dirt fifteen feet in the air. Digging was not the answer. We just lay there while the enemy adjusted fire on us. We tried to figure where their FO was located, but we had no clue. They either ran out of rounds or just gave up before anyone in Bravo was hurt.

At noon the CO called a staff meeting. He had received a coded message from Battalion. The enemy was indeed massing. Bravo and Charlie were to return to Battalion immediately. We would move in thirty minutes and head due east, spread out in a fighting formation: two platoons up and one back. The CO specifically told us that everyone was to use full camouflage. We did not have much greasepaint available, but we all cut brush and vegetation and jammed it into our web gear. When we pulled out, Bravo Company looked like a walking cornfield or something. Battalion CP was barely three thousand meters away.

We moved out, still expecting to run into something. For the last four or five weeks the enemy seemed to know where we were most of the time. They had spent the morning adjusting artillery fire on us, but somehow they must have lost track of Bravo Company. Maybe it was the camouflage.

The NVA was massing, all right. One NVA battalion had spread out and settled in about a thousand meters west of 1/5's location. They were facing east, and the last thing they must have expected was that a Marine Corps rifle company would walk up their backsides. In another twist that may have really worked to our benefit that afternoon, the first man to die that day would be their battalion commander.

Bravo Company's CP group is moving between the two front platoons about one hundred meters back. 2d Platoon is following us by about one hundred meters. We move off a shelf and down through a dry creek bed, up over the top, and out into open, broken country. The

CP group of perhaps fifteen or twenty of us then moves diagonally north, up onto a small hill.

We have been moving for less than an hour. The right flank squad of the right front platoon is moving 150 meters ahead and to our right front along a low retaining wall, next to several deserted huts. Suddenly an NVA in khaki uniform walks out of a bunker hidden under one of the hooches. As he steps into daylight, he sees a line of Marines walking about thirty feet away on the retaining wall. He draws a 9mm pistol from his belt and shoots a Marine, center chest, through an open flak jacket. Several Marines fire back at once, blowing the NVA officer almost in half and his body back down the bunker entrance in a dead heap.

We hear the shooting and see the line of Marines drop down behind the low wall. Immediately a fight breaks out between the Marines there and an undetermined number of enemy hidden in and around the hooches.

Before we can react to the action, we take automatic fire from somewhere behind and below us. We all hit the deck, but because we are up on the side of the hill, our profiles are still up even when we lie down. The firing at us continues. Several weapons are shooting at once, and bullets are flying all around. Every good war story has the same incident: The men on either side of me are hit. The Marine on my right takes a bullet through the left arm. The Marine on my left gets hit in the right thigh. And the shooting continues.

We cannot stay put, but there is no place to go. If something doesn't happen quickly, we will take a lot of casualties. With wounded on each side of me, I pull out my only bandage and begin to help the two casualties. I call for a corpsman, but with bullets filling the air, no one responds. It may be only seconds, but it seems like an eternity. Bullets are hitting the ground and snapping past me in the air.

The 2d Platoon sees the NVA open fire on us, and without an order the platoon breaks into skirmish lines and attacks. Marines moving across open ground at first receive heavy return fire. One Marine is hit in the heart. He moans and pitches forward, dead. Three more Marines are hit, but the attack continues. The platoon is firing and walking. They shoot several NVA in their fox-holes and then take out the automatic weapon.

The NVA do what they sometimes do when they are surprised: They break. Many drop their weapons and run. The Marines press the attack and kill twenty-five or thirty enemy soldiers in a matter of minutes.

Meanwhile, back on the hill, we are relieved. With the shooting stopped, heads begin to pop up. The corpsman shows up. I am pumped up on adrenaline and scared half to death. When I see the corpsman, I almost yell at him, "The next time I call for a corpsman and you don't show, I will put a bullet in your ass and medevac you to Da Nang." It is really uncalled for, but I have been the only one up during the shooting and now I am on a roll.

The fighting is going on now in every direction. We do not know it yet, but we are in their midst. Shouting comes from the top of our hill. I grab the radio and run to the top. Four hundred meters away, on top of the next hill, four NVA are carrying a heavy machine gun with a tripod. Halfway down our hill, five Marines take off in that direction at a dead run. They are trying to get close enough to stop the gun crew before that machine gun is working.

I am on the radio calling for an AO. At that moment

a Cobra attack helicopter checks in. He is close, and we throw out a smoke grenade. He finds us quickly, and we talk him over to the NVA gun crew. The five Marines are halfway up the enemy's hill when the Cobra rolls in. The enemy gun crew has selected a spot, and all four NVA are busily trying to get the gun going before the Marines arrive.

The Cobra fires a long burst from its 7.62mm Gatling gun. We can see the impacting rounds move from east to west and right through the gun crew. Two of the NVA just fall back over dead, but two of them hop like crickets, about a foot off the ground, and drop dead. Fifteen seconds later the Marines top the hill. Without the Cobra it would have been close.

We use the Cobras all that afternoon. The F-4s and the Cobras shoot a lot of rockets, but the two sides are mixed together and we cannot use bombs or napalm. With the fighting so close and aircraft circling around, we never shoot artillery.

I really have to love the job the Cobras do today.

The Cobra is a wonderful weapons system. Really, a *magnificent* weapons system. Aside from the 7.62mm Gatling gun, it carries an automatic 40mm grenade launcher and either 2.75-inch or 3.5-inch Zuni rockets. We are engaging targets within ten meters of friendly troops, "danger/close, ten meters," all afternoon, and have no friendly casualties. It is really exciting. I work like a clearinghouse for targets, talking with Marines on the ground and transferring information to the aircraft. When it comes to close coordinated supporting fire, the Marine Corps invented it, and is the best in the world.

Bravo Company has sustained one dead and ten wounded from hostile fire, and they all need to get out.

Aside from the two wounded we have at the company CP, two more are with 1st Platoon, about one hundred meters east of us. The dead Marine and now six wounded Marines are about three hundred meters to our southwest. We must consolidate.

We call 1st Platoon and tell them we will bring our two WIAs (wounded in action) to their location and set up one LZ there. The second LZ will be west of the village. We help our two wounded down to the east end of the hill. Just as we reach the bottom, we find a black communications wire lying across the trail. Marines are carefully stepping over it. It would be smart to cut the line, but I have two wounded and random firing is all around. I just keep going and no one ever cuts it. It turns out later to be the enemy's main communications line.

We are at the end. Ahead of us is one hundred meters of open paddy to the trees and 1st Platoon. A firefight rages back and forth across a wide, open paddy to our south 150 meters. The fight is between the six Marines down behind the retaining wall and an unknown number of NVA trapped in the hooches and bunkers in the village. The Marines now have support from part of 2d Platoon.

When the Marines behind the wall start to fire, we will go. I will take the Marine with the arm wound first. The bone in his upper left arm is broken and protruding; his wound is the more serious.

The Marines at the wall begin to fire. I put the WIA's right arm around my neck, with my left hand I grab his cartridge belt, and we run like hell. He is running on a dike and I am several inches lower at ground level. Still I have no trouble staying up with him. For five or six seconds the fire is all going out.

Now there is a lot of return fire. They say you never hear the bullet that hits you. I still don't know. I am running too hard to listen anyway. About halfway across, my man stumbles. We have his left arm strapped across his chest. When he stumbles, he has no way to catch himself. I have his right arm around my neck and am holding him tightly. He almost pulls me down, too. We stop. The shooting is still heavy. I feel very exposed. He says, "Let's go!" quite impatiently. He is game but becoming weak. We start to run again. I don't want him to go into shock before we get across. Finally we make the trees. There is a corpsman waiting for him.

The Marines have already designated an LZ north of the trees, kind of stuck out in a paddy. I do not argue with them. I still have another casualty back at the Bravo CP. The Marines at the wall open fire, and I take off running on the dike. By myself the return trip is much easier, but there is a lot of shooting.

I do not even see the skipper back at the CP. We still have fighting in three directions, and he is busy. I would be happy for someone else to make the next trip, but no one offers. The Marine with the leg wound is called Pops. He is thirty-one years old or so, hence the nickname; he's from a small town in the Midwest. The story goes that he had been married to the daughter of a prominent family. She apparently found someone she liked better and asked for a divorce. He argued with her about it and immediately was drafted and gone. He decided that if he had to go anyway, he wanted to go with the best, and so he asked to be a Marine. He found everyone eager to let him.

Pops is hit in the right thigh. The bullet punctured a can of 7-Up he had nursed for two days, passed through the thigh muscle, and exited cleanly. Bandaged and in some pain, he seems pretty up, considering the circumstances. He says, "This is golden. I have less than four months to do, so I won't be back. They'll send me home."

When the Marines at the wall begin to shoot, Pops takes off like a deer. I had grabbed him by the cartridge belt, not knowing what to expect. For the first several strides it seems I may be holding him back. I am running low again and have to pump hard to catch up. I know someone is shooting at us, but I am not hearing or sensing anything. We just run as hard as we can.

In fact, the firing at us is lighter. By this third exchange of fire the Marines at the wall are beginning to take a toll on the NVA they were engaging. Several enemy soldiers have already been shot. One NVA makes the mistake of repeating his pattern of fire too often. The Marines notice that when they fire, he does the same thing each time. A Marine sneaks over the wall and hides underneath the window from where the enemy is firing. The Marines at the wall fire, and when the enemy soldier shows himself at the window again, the Marine crouching below grabs the enemy's rifle barrel and jams a K-bar through his chest. He drags the NVA out through the window and finishes killing him.

Pops does finally begin to slow, and I do finally help him make it. I was expecting more of a struggle to get him across. We have called for a medevac, but I did not bring the radio this trip because I did not want to fight it and Pops together. So I have to make one more trip for the radio. I make it back easily enough, as there is only sporadic firing either way.

The choppers are already headed our way, so I need to

hurry back. But on my fifth trip across the paddy that afternoon, I begin to seriously run out of gas. I tell myself to ignore the pain. "You cannot stop. You do not even want to slow down." I am blowing hard and beginning to wobble.

About ten meters short of the trees, my left foot slips off the right side of the dike. I make an awkward kind of half turn on one leg and fall backward spread-eagled. I have the radio over one shoulder and manage to hold on to it. I land flat on my back, and for a brief moment it feels safe just to be down. Before I can even collect myself, two Marines run out from the trees and grab me through the shoulder holes of my flak jacket. They head back to the trees with such a jerk that everything but my heels comes off the ground.

Quickly we arrive back at the trees, and they drop me. The way I went down, most thought I had been shot. I convince them that all I need is air, and I lie there puffing until I can finally catch my breath again.

The choppers report in, and I make my way to the other end of the tree line. We have set out two LZs, and we have two CH-46s available to us.

An enemy .30-caliber automatic weapon is reportedly located two hundred meters east across a large paddy. I call the choppers and tell them the problem.

"Be sure you come in from the south or west. Do not approach from the north or east. Over."

The pilot calls back confirmation: "Roger."

We have air panels set out. The pilot confirms that he can see the panels. Now, a screwup. Someone in the trees behind us throws yellow smoke.

I cannot say enough about the courage that the pilots, especially the chopper pilots, display on a daily basis.

When Marines are in trouble on the ground, the pilots do incredible things to help us out. But this pilot is trying too hard and not listening enough. When he sees the smoke trailing north, he rolls in from that direction.

It is too late to wave him off; he is coming fast. He will be sixty or seventy feet away and rolling left to right. We grab up our wounded and start to run for the descending bird. The chopper touches down and is rolling across our front. As we all approach the craft, the crew chief begins to wave frantically from the rear of the bird.

We have just reached the chopper and I notice the sides of the helicopter beginning to perforate as projectiles pierce both skins. The chopper never stops rolling. The nose lifts, and our bird takes off and flies away. We hit the deck. The enemy's automatic weapon cannot shoot at us directly, but almost can. We have to painfully crawl with our wounded back to the trees.

Once we can stand, I eyeball the line of sight and set up an LZ behind the trees. We put out air panels. This time the pilots will approach the way we tell them to. No smoke. The second chopper comes in from the south, high over the village. It drops very fast coming across the paddy and barely clears our trees. The pilot sets it down immediately and we must scatter to make room. Curb service. It takes only seconds to load the wounded. The bird rolls and is gone.

Now for the second zone. "I say again: Approach from the south or west. Do not approach from the east." I call the other zone to be sure they are ready. Their panels are out and no one will throw smoke. Instead of heading directly to Da Nang, the chopper with the wounded continues to climb and swings from north to east and then back south.

We have only one emergency wound: the first Marine to be shot that day on the wall by the NVA battalion commander. He was shot center chest, and the bullet entered just under his sternum, passed cleanly through his body, and exited, missing the spine by fractions of an inch. For an hour he has no feeling or movement in his legs. His platoon cuts a pole and straps him to it with belts to immobilize his back. By now, though, he is full of morphine, and movement is returning to his extremities. He is telling jokes and talking about home.

There is no good place for 2d Platoon to set up an LZ. From the tree line on the east, which the enemy most definitely controls, it is three hundred meters of mostly open ground to the village. From the village to the west, it is all wide open. They have set up the LZ about three hundred meters west of the village. Our best hope is that it will be far enough to the west.

The chopper that was shot out of the first zone already has a number of holes through it. I cannot believe it when he comes rolling in from the east. He is only two hundred feet in the air on a long, slow descent toward the second zone. When he clears the tree line on the east, an automatic weapon starts up. He still has six hundred meters to go. No way.

We all hold our breath as we watch the chopper cover the first three hundred meters. "Come on, baby." The bird is a hundred feet high when the blades suddenly seem to lose torque. A CH-46 must be made of 90 percent air; that chopper had twenty or thirty bullets pass through it before one finally hit a hydraulic line. The aircraft drops like a rock, hits hard about one hundred meters short of the LZ, bounces two or three times, and keeps rolling. All of a sudden there is a lot of yelling on all of the radios.

The chopper already carrying wounded never hesitates. He makes a short, banking turn. In order to pull this off, he must approach parallel, from behind the downed chopper. He is already high, and the pilot makes another breathtaking descent straight down over the village. The crew from the downed chopper has bailed out and is crouched down behind it for cover.

The rescue chopper hits the ground hard and bounces high in the air. It hits again and barely bounces. It begins to roll alongside the crippled ship, and the second crew jumps up and dives through the windows.

The pilot covers the remaining distance to the LZ, lifting up hardly at all. He sets the CH-46 down again, and Marines in the LZ literally throw the wounded through the windows. That includes our emergency case, who finds himself launched headfirst like a javelin through a window. The chopper never stops rolling, and then he is gone. He has picked up one dead, ten wounded, and a downed aircrew that is very tightly puckered. If anyone ever deserved a flying medal, it is that guy.

We spent the afternoon using the Cobras to bust up hard targets and soften resistance. The fighting became more static. Marines were consolidating, shooting into holes and blowing bunkers, either digging NVA out or trying to bury them in place. There is no question that we were in the middle of something that day, and that beaucoup NVA were all around.

The NVA could not move during the daytime without us whacking them hard. But it was getting late, and they would not be afraid to move at night. It was time to get things in order. The CO took one platoon and went to the downed chopper to strip it. They retrieved the waist guns and any papers or maps, and destroyed the radios.

The rest of the company began to clean up and count. We had captured seventy rifles and pistols, including another very nice silver-plated 9mm with pearl handles. We wondered if it was the mate to the one we had taken two days prior, during the alley cat. We also captured some heavy weapons, the finest of which was a 12.7mm with tripod. It was a frightening gun just to look at. In all, we counted seventy-five dead NVA and almost eighty weapons. We captured additional enemy information, including a map with unit locations marked on it. And in the process we had gutted an NVA battalion. We had one dead Marine and ten wounded. Bravo 1/5 was cleaning up from a very good day indeed.

The company consolidated on a hill across from the village. It was getting dark. When the CO returned from the downed helicopter, we buried the captured arms and the waist guns on the hill. It took an hour or more.

The top of every hill in Vietnam had a 500-pound bomb crater on it. Twenty feet in diameter at the top, they were conelike down to a point about twelve feet deep, like giant doodlebug holes. This hill was no different. You quickly learn that if you are on top of a hill and put a strobe light in the bottom of the crater, the light can be seen only from the air. It makes a great beacon, around which you can direct air support while everything still looks black from the ground.

The NVA begins to show up in large numbers an hour after dark. Below us is loud talking and what sounds like pipes or pieces of metal being banged together. Perhaps they are gathering to the sound of the metal banging. It crosses my mind that they may be trying to rally. I begin to wonder how we will ever get off this hill. But if the NVA know we are up here, they give no immediate indication. We put out a strobe, and while the company finishes burying its cache, my FAC team calls in a Spooky gunship to entertain the NVA.

We had a lot of great weapons available to us. Americans are a resourceful bunch. One of the most awesome weapons was the Spooky gunship. Its official name was Puff the Magic Dragon. We called the gunships Spooky because that is exactly what they were. These converted World War II air force C-47 transports each had a battery of three 7.62mm Gatling guns at the left waist, each six-barrel gun capable of firing one hundred rounds a second. The pilot aimed through a sight mounted on the wing. Up in the darkness, unseen, the pilot flew in left-hand circles, lined up the sights, and fired bursts, sometimes long bursts, at a target area. If you were the enemy, you did not want to fire any tracers into the air while Spooky was around. If so, you might have that long tongue of fire lick down to the ground and kiss you goodnight. Spooky could also drop flares if you wanted light. But on that night, I was happy in the darkness.

Bravo was in a tight little circle.

We gave Spooky a direction south from the strobe and told him to fire a burst at an area one hundred to two hundred meters from us. It took him almost a minute to line us up. When he started to fire, we heard not only the usual *brrrrr* of the gun itself but also the sound of the bullets rushing through the air just over our heads. It was both frightening and reassuring. The response on the ground was incredible, too. Instantly we heard a loud, shrill scream. Voices yelled in Vietnamese, and just screamed. The banging of metal became frantic.

"You got 'em, baby. Hose them down." The Spooky worked around for the next hour. The party below us broke up and the night became quiet. We'll never know if Spooky hit anything that night, but he did seem to cause a lot of excitement. An hour later, word came that we were pulling out.

We were still about fifteen hundred meters from Battalion and did not want to be anywhere around here in the morning. As we picked up our gear, word came that the CO wanted me. I found him down near the east end of the hill. Marines were quietly forming up in the darkness and checking their weapons. I had to get close to see him. He had the two snipers with him and was holding his map down at his side. When I got close, he said, "Listen, I am so exhausted I can't even think. Would you take the point and get the company back to Battalion?" I could imagine that he was exhausted. He should be.

Although I was the next senior officer to the captain, he had three platoon commanders who could have taken us back. I was surprised he had called me, and frankly I was flattered.

We put a poncho over us, turned on a flashlight, and turned the map around to orient ourselves. I pulled out my compass and shined the light on it to charge up the dial. We agreed on a direction, and he added, "Take the two snipers in case we run into something."

A young Marine once told me that his greatest thrill as a Marine was to walk point for an entire rifle battalion kicking off an operation. Though I lived like a grunt for most of my tour, I was an 0800, an artillery officer. I never really considered myself a grunt. When it came to walking point for the company that night, thrilling would be a good word for it. I was pumped. Even though the FAC team had accounted for a full third of the enemy dead, I had not fired a weapon all day.

We would walk through an area that had lots of NVA, but I felt up to the job. In a war of attrition, Bravo had experienced a good day. I was still pumped up, and now I would fight, take a bullet, do anything to get Bravo Company back to Battalion. That night I was a grunt.

Walking point that night was one of my proudest moments as a Marine. It ranks with the day in Quantico when I picked up my sword. Maybe having the snipers close by made me braver, too. Although I am certain that we walked right past enemy soldiers that night, we saw no one and had no problems while finding our way back. When we got close, Battalion fired a flare and we made it back to our lines without incident. Perhaps the enemy had seen enough of Bravo Company for one day.

We entered the lines and took up the southern one-third of the low hill that we would call home for a while. It should go without saying that Battalion was happy to see us. We received a quiet but hearty homecoming. Everyone else in the battalion wanted to know what had happened, and over the next few days everyone in Bravo Company got to tell his story at least once. We were hot. We were studs.

The next morning the CO told me that Alpha Company, along with him and several Marines from Bravo, were going back to yesterday's fight scene. They would help a CH-64 Skycrane helicopter from Da Nang lift out the downed chopper and would also dig up the weapons and other booty and bring it all back to Battalion. Some of the Marines from Bravo were going back because they had buried some prizes separately. The CO asked me if I wanted to tag along. The FAC leader and another battalion staffer were going along, too, so I stayed put.

That place had far too many enemy soldiers skulking around who were far too aggressive for my liking.

Two days later a cable arrived: "From: The Commandant of The Marine Corps, Washington, D.C. To: Headquarters, Bravo Company. Congratulations. Your actions on June 7, 1969, resulting in twenty-six enemy dead, without sustaining any friendly casualties, was in the proudest traditions," etc., etc. From the freaking commandant! Our lifer had himself a real prize. He deserved it. I served with two company commanders while in Vietnam, and they were both very sharp.

So, there we were. Our location was too long to be a hill and too low to be a hogback.

The battalion was now in a tight little circle around an elliptical terrain feature no more than twenty feet high, about two hundred meters long north and south, and seventy-five meters wide east and west. It had a few scraggly trees, lots of craters big and small, and lots of dirt. We were backed up two hundred meters from the river, just across from An Hoa.

Word came from Regiment that the NVA had two thousand troops facing us. Their mission was to eliminate 1/5 and press on to An Hoa. Our battalion S-3 sent a defiant message back to Regiment stating that, upon being informed of the new intelligence report, the battalion commander had said, "Good! Now I have them where I want them." What he may have actually said was, "How do we get these damned pigs back across the river?" (referring to the two APCs and the almost vertical banks of the river).

It was about June 10. We stayed right there for the next six weeks, until the last week of July. And the enemy would attack us every other night, just like clockwork. A battle with no name at a place with no name—quite common in the annals of warfare. After all these years, only the survivors remember. At the time, we did not know what to expect. I am hopeful that Regiment, or someone, had a better perspective on all this than I did.

At that point the war was really getting close to me, and I wanted out. Death and dying were everywhere, and much too common for sanity. The fighting can only get so close so many times, and sooner or later your luck runs out. I only had to talk to John to find reinforcement. We had fought the fight. We had done our duty. Now we wanted the fuck out.

We did not know then that we would be in that battleground for six weeks; we only knew that we were there. Until someone somewhere else changed his mind, we would stay right there in the dirt. We were going to kill them, or they were going to kill us. Like a piece of bait with its own set of teeth, 1/5 was hung out for the enemy.

Death has a smell to it. Actually, it has two smells to it. Blood has a distinctive odor. I have described it as smelling like iron. It is the smell of fresh kill. After twelve to twenty-four hours, depending on sun and moisture, all that's left is rotting meat. I have heard that described as a sickly sweet smell. That is as good as I can describe it. Some things you just don't forget.

In close combat your attention and your focus become very short-term and quite immediate. Getting attacked every other night, the battalion quickly found itself running on a forty-eight-hour clock, and for the first week or ten days I was very scared all the time.

I had been at war a long time, and by this point in my tour I had seen a lot. Fear was much more common than good food, and I will tell you freely that I was scared. We talked about it, hoping to reassure one another, but fear was always close to the surface. The fighting would happen only at night.

We'd go through forty or so hours of anxious waiting, resting, and distracting. As soon as the fighting began, I actually felt better. You remember quickly that in combat, everything is relative. If they are shooting at you, the fighting is bad. If they are shooting at someone else, the fighting is not so bad.

Proving that a person can adapt to anything, I became accustomed to it after the first ten days. On one level you are still terrified, but in everything you do, life becomes normal. The fear becomes so common that you almost forget it. Your survival instinct becomes quite discerning. The shooting goes there, the shooting comes here; only when the shooting became really bad did I consciously feel the fear.

On three different nights the enemy breached our lines, and Marines had to hunt them down and kill them among us. On several other nights they got close to or into our lines, but night after night we stopped them one way or another. We had the 105s and the 155s shooting from An Hoa. We dropped napalm and 250-pound bombs and fired rockets. And anytime we wanted a Spooky, we only had to ask. We had phenomenal firepower, and in the summer of 1969, 1/5 was a pretty tough unit.

Still, they came. You had to respect them. They had

less of everything, and they overcame incredible hard-
ships and obstacles to push themselves in front of our
guns. At the time I did not deeply question it. They
would come and we would kill as many as we could.
Then we would rest while they resupplied. Then they
would come again. But remember, this was not Gettys-
burg; this was Vietnam. There were two thousand NVA
with a half dozen big mortars, a couple of recoilless rifles, and what at times seemed like an awful lot of automatic weapons of various sizes. They were matched
against five hundred Marines, reinforced from about
one mile away by the entire United States of America.
We should have held them.

In return for the casualties we inflicted on the enemy,
seventeen Marines died and another two dozen were
wounded. Seven of the dead were friendly fire. We took
five hundred Marines to the Arizona Territory, and in
eighty days we killed six hundred NVA. I am sure that is
not a record, but in a war of attrition it is pretty good.
They were courageous, determined fighters, but we had
awesome firepower.

I saw some great shots in Vietnam.

We have been in place less than forty-eight hours. I
walk down the west slope of the hill to a clump of trees
in order to find our front positions. As I approach, the
senior sniper waves me down to the front of the trees.
He has a ship's glass down there and is eyeballing for
targets. He says, "Lieutenant, look what we found.
We're just waiting."

I look through the glass to see part of a hooch with a
cooking fire going out front. The junior sniper and a
new 0301 (second lieutenant, platoon commander) are

here, too. They think that if they watch that fire, they will find a target. They have already calculated the distance. I look at their map, and it appears to be at or just over one thousand meters.

The new platoon commander is looking through the glass when he suddenly almost shouts with excitement, "There's someone now!"

The sniper holds the .270-caliber scoped target rifle out to me. "You want him?"

I take it as a compliment, and I will kill him if I have to. As a practical matter, someone needs to kill this guy while we have him there. Better than facing him tomorrow night when he is armed and ready. But others are ready for the job. I pass, so the new lieutenant says, "Can I take him?" He has been in-country less than a month and is anxious to make his bones.

I peer through the glass. A khaki uniform bends over the fire, stirring a pot. He stands up to speak to someone. The .270 cracks. The khaki stumbles backward a step and then pitches forward next to the fire, still.

Immediately a young Vietnamese male about fourteen years old and dressed in black pajama bottoms and top darts into the field of vision. He grabs the khaki uniform and tries to drag the downed NVA away. The new lieutenant is still looking through the scope and says, "Oh, look at this." I hear the sniper snatch the rifle from the young officer's hands and slam the bolt. After that it takes no more than three or four seconds. Black pajamas is pulling furiously but has moved only a few feet. The .270 cracks again. Black pajamas staggers back a step and falls on top of the khaki. Now they are both still.

Two in a pile at a thousand meters. I think that is pretty good shooting. A sniper's bullet costs thirteen cents, and Marine Corps snipers are referred to as the "thirteen-cent killers" for good reason.

I learned to hate the mortars. Machine guns are bad enough, but if you lie down flat, a machine gun may have trouble hitting you. Mortar rounds come straight down. Getting into a hole may not be helpful. You hear the round coming about one-half second before it detonates. Not enough time to even flinch. Mortars are not always a fast death, either. Ten or fifteen nickel-sized puncture wounds may bleed you to death, but it can take a while.

Some nights the enemy walked mortar rounds back and forth on the long axis of our lines. Some nights he tried to drop them all in one small area. On most nights the shooting and the detonations would come close to my position at some point. On at least three occasions I really believed that I would take a hit. A voice in my head would say, "This is it. . . . This is it." But each time it was not me.

My gear took a beating during these attacks. Anything exposed on the ground ended up looking like Swiss cheese, and forget about keeping an air mattress.

Facing your mortality, believing that you are about to die, can change the way you feel about life. I did not come to any flash of wisdom or deep personal insight from the experience. I can readily tell you that I developed a lifelong appreciation for seeing the sun rise.

I was always happy to see first light. By first light it was over, for a while. You could heat up a morning brew and think about lima beans for breakfast.

John's post was with Charlie Company at the north end of the hill. We met in the middle at the battalion CP from time to time to catch up. It seemed clear that John was feeling as pressed as I was about all the shooting going on. I was superstitious about counting the time left on my tour while still in the bush. But anyone could count from the end of September until the end of July and get ten months. That meant we were getting short. When an 0800 gets short, he is supposed to go back to a battery or into a bunker, isn't he? Well, John and I were getting restless. Marines had a saying for when things got tough: "I was too short for this shit when I got here." We had been "here," in the dirt, for four or five weeks, and we wanted out.

We were commiserating at Battalion one afternoon when the idea of stealing one of the "pigs" and making a dash for the river came up, only half jokingly. The idea of cranking up one of the APCs in the middle of the night was so funny that we both laughed. We got started laughing and we could not stop. We laughed until we cried. We both felt better for a while.

July 21, 1969. The battalion was still sitting and wondering. Fighting was tapering off. The enemy was still around in large numbers, but he seemed less willing to use his troops. Sometime that afternoon the battalion radio squawked to life. "All stations this net be advised; the United States has landed a man on the moon. I say again, an American is walking on the moon. Out."

Several Marines were close enough to get the news. It was daytime, but the moon was clearly visible in the sky. We sat there, looking up. It seemed incredible to me that another American was up there on the moon, looking back. It really made me feel proud to be an American.

After a moment of silence, Al Thayer, one of the RTOs (radiotelephone operators), said, "If Uncle can send a man half a million miles to the moon and back, why can't somebody get my ass out of Vietnam?" I hope Al became an accountant; he had an eye for the bottom line.

Shortly thereafter, word came that the siege was broken. The enemy was retreating. Someone somewhere had decided that enough was enough for now.

All the lifers at Battalion wanted to press the edge. They argued strongly that if two companies formed up and attacked now, we could overrun the enemy's retrograde and cheaply score additional kills. I was glad to hear that the battalion CO said no. He had been sent to do a job and had succeeded handily. He seemed happy to be headed back to An Hoa.

He could not have been as happy as I was. Word came that John and I would catch a chopper to Da Nang the next day. We were going to get out, after all, the first thing the next morning.

I had become quite blasé about the fighting. If the enemy wanted me to move, they had to shoot right at me, directly. So that night they walked mortar rounds right through my position and my gear. I crashed into the bottom of our 500-pound bomb crater at a dead run. My heart was pounding, and multiple rounds were hitting all at once. When it passed, I was in the bottom, in a pile of garbage, head down. I managed to right myself and claw my way back to the top.

The next morning everything was better, except I had a cut on my forearm that kept bleeding. It had come at the bottom of the crater, from an old C-ration can.

When my corpsman saw it, he insisted on cleaning the cut and treating it like a wound. I might have gotten a Purple Heart if I had tried. I was feeling wounded all right, but two Marines had really been wounded that night. I was just lucky not to earn a Purple Heart, too.

6

Getting Short

Give me my freedom
for as long as I be
All I ask of livin'
is to have no chains on me
All I ask of livin'
is to have no chains on me
And all I ask of dyin' is to
go naturally, only wanna
go naturally
Here I go!
hey hey
Here come the devil
right behind
—Blood, Sweat and Tears, "And When I Die"

John Juracek and I reported in to 7th Marines regimental CP, picked up our orders and our gear, and caught a chopper to the bright lights, Da Nang. Division looked much the same. Most of the debris and damage had been cleared away from the last time the ammo dump had blown up. But somehow the charm was gone. We landed and caught a ride up to division HQ and reported in to G-1 (personnel).

Immediately, things began to look up. The G-1 for 1st Marine Division was my old battalion commander, Lieutenant Colonel Quinn. He called me Bill, shook my hand, and told us to take five days off and go to Okinawa for a rest. Life was looking good.

Before I left for Okinawa, I ran into Lee Neely. He

had finished his bush time with Mike Company and rotated back to Division. He was working for Quinn in
G-1, and his particular niche was editing the meritorious
commendations as they moved up the chain. He told me
he had seen my name recently, but because he had not
expected to see me again, he could not remember what
it involved. I could not imagine what I had done meritorious, so I forgot about it. The rest of the news was bad.
Both John Mason and Tom Harrell had been hit, hard.

Mason's platoon had used a bangalore torpedo to
clear a hedgerow of mines. Despite this, John was standing next to a Marine who stepped on a large mine. The
Marine was killed and John took extensive shrapnel
wounds to his right side. He lost his right calf muscle,
and his right elbow had to be welded solid at an angle.

Tom Harrell had been hit recently and brought to Da
Nang. His platoon had just bedded down when a VC
fired a single antitank round. It detonated a few feet in
front of Tom's upper torso and he took shrapnel in both
eyes. He lost one eye completely and 60 percent sight in
the other. His right arm and shoulder suffered extensive
damage. His elbow would be welded, too.

Lee took me to see Tom in the hospital at Da Nang
before he was shipped out to another. He was taking it
as well as could be expected. "No hill for a climber," he
reminded me. I was always surprised by the high level of
morale that our wounded exhibited. He had the wound,
and I was the one getting angry.

Juracek and I managed to catch a C-130 flight the
next morning. Okinawa was sunny and laid back. For
five days we lay around the AOQ (air officers quarters).
We ate their food and sucked up their alcohol and air-
conditioning. It was hot in Okinawa, of course, but de-

spite that we made it to town each day for a sauna and a rubdown.

On one trip we were riding in a civilian bus full of Americans when traffic was blocked by a street demonstration. A large crowd was doing a dragon dance through the street. Chanters with bullhorns were chanting anti-American slogans.

Our bus stopped along with everyone else; there was no way off and nowhere to go. John and I became apprehensive, but one of the navy personnel said, "Don't move, and don't look out of the bus." We sat and read a *Stars and Stripes* while the dragon pounded on the bus as it passed. It took four or five minutes, and then traffic began to move again.

By the time we got back to Da Nang, it was August 1. That left us with eighty-seven days until October 26. Come on, eighty-six! We reported in to 11th Marines, and they split us up to help plug holes around the regiment.

I was sent to an 8-inch platoon on the east side of Da Nang. When I checked in, they were happy to see me. I was not assigned to the FDC. Instead, I became the catch-all officer for the unit. I was assigned about five billets, including motor pool, fire safety, and anything that had to be done that no one wanted to do. The previous battery commander had built a handball court, so for most of three weeks I played handball with an Aggie from San Angelo, Texas. The food was hot, they had ice, and the PX (post exchange) was only ten minutes away. I easily could have ended my tour right there and finished with a kick, but someone at Regiment found another hole for me to plug. I became the regimental R&R officer.

During the next two or three weeks, I was shipped to two different artillery units that had officers taking their week of R&R. My first stop was with a Marine unit reinforcing our allies the Koreans.

Let me say it again: Vietnam is beautiful. We had a three-truck convoy pulling out of 11th Marines. We turned south through the dirty streets of partly military, partly civilian chaos and drove down to a spot where the road ran out onto the beach. The trucks took a right, and we proceeded to drive along fifteen miles of the most beautiful, most magnificent, perfectly white, perfectly wonderful beach your mind can imagine. The water was absolutely clear. We drove past camps and villages. Cooking fires were going and civilians were fishing. The water and sand were pristine, and the scene was idyllic. It was a beautiful tropical day and people were living on the beach. It was so perfect. Who would ever want to live in any other place?

The Marine Corps had, or perhaps still has, a Rube Goldberg kind of contraption they called an artillery piece. It was an APC with an old vertical-breech 105mm howitzer jammed inside. Only in the Marine Corps. These were developed for fighting in the island campaigns of World War II. If the fighting is very close and you are concerned about snipers or projectiles cutting the crew down, then this is the answer. They had a relatively high rate of fire, and they were intimidating monsters. They were also hellishly hot, very old, and so crowded that you could not imagine any of the crew surviving the recoil. Still, we had them in our armory, so we sent them to support the ROKs.

The Koreans had a pretty good deal for themselves. The Korean government participated in Vietnam and helped fight communism, but was willing to send volunteers only. In order to be sure of enough volunteers, the U.S. government was willing to provide an incentive. While American soldiers received a combat bonus of sixty-five dollars each month for hazardous duty, the U.S. government matched the entire base pay for each Korean soldier who volunteered. And while they were known to be excellent fighters, any Korean company commander who began to take "too many" casualties was rotated home. As a result, the Korean troops sometimes lacked "aggressiveness."

Our APC-carried 105s were a part of their camp. We provided them with artillery support and relied on them for water, rations, electricity, sanitation, and just about everything else. A lot of little rubs occurred between the allies. They were supposed to pick up our trash twice a week, as they did for the rest of the camp. They seldom picked up our trash at all, and when it got bad and we complained, they cut off our electricity. We finally had to remind them that the next fire mission we shot might hit an ROK unit if the FDC had no lights.

I met a great number of very sharp people in the Marine Corps. This battery had a gunnery sergeant who was not yet thirty years old. He had chiseled features and bright eyes, a recruiter's dream. He said something to a group of us that almost sounded absurd under the circumstances, but proved to be prophetic. While talking one evening after chow, he said that if peace happened to break out tomorrow, if tomorrow morning we woke up to find the Soviet Union had vanished and peace reigned throughout the world, America would still need the Marine Corps.

He said that young people need both a challenge and

a positive force in their lives in order to succeed. The Marine Corps not only provides both of those for personal growth, but also teaches a young person how to dress, present himself, and how to devise, organize, and execute a plan. Even if there is no external threat to our national security, he contended, America will always need new leaders, and the Marine Corps will always provide them. Those words came back to me years later as I watched television and saw the Berlin Wall come down.

My next stop was at the 8-inch platoon back in An Hoa. They were rebuilding their gun pits for better drainage, and I spent a week helping them dig, move dirt, and try to improve the drainage. It may have been only a coincidence, but during that week we had no attacks by the enemy, and no incoming, either.

I went into the camp one day and was walking past 5th Marines CP. There, sitting out front, was a captured 12.7mm antiaircraft weapon sitting on a tripod. I looked at the sign hanging on it. CAPTURED BY 1ST BATTALION, 5TH MARINES. It was the antiaircraft gun that Bravo had taken during that long afternoon in June on our way to join Battalion. I felt a twinge of pride and a kind of historical significance. It had been almost three months.

An Hoa never did have any appeal for me. The enemy may have been licking his wounds for a while, but he would be back. I was happy to finish my week.

I was ready for Da Nang and was beginning to feel "short." It was the first week of September, and "the count" was under sixty days. Back in the World, the first American troop withdrawals had been announced. America was beginning to quit, and some army units were starting to pull back.

When I reached Da Nang, I was immediately reassigned to a 175mm gun platoon. I arrived as they were loading up to move out to support the Green Beret firebase at Thong Duc. One of our rifle battalions had already moved to the firebase and begun patrols.

If the 8-inch howitzer looks like a hog, the 175mm gun looks like a giraffe, with its long, slender barrel tapering down almost to a point. It fires a 200-pound projectile and has a range of thirty-five kilometers (that's over twenty miles). We would be the only artillery support that could reach Thong Duc. We loaded up and moved out in a long armored convoy bristling with weapons.

Many army units fought bravely in Vietnam. But during my three years in the Marine Corps, I never heard the United States Army referred to as anything but "the dog ass army." It was the draft army, fighting what many draftees felt was an unjust war in a place they did not belong.

We, on the other hand, were volunteers, fighting because our country was at war. We had no use for them, and they hated us. I mean, they absolutely *hated* us. The army seemed to have a great deal more animosity for the Marine Corps than they had for the enemy. Knowing that Marines were moving in behind them, the army destroyed everything they could at the firebase.

Tearing the doors off was not enough. They rammed their trucks into the sides of bunkers and used chains to pull things apart. They had to go far out of their way to do that kind of damage. Virtually everything bad you have heard about the draftee army in Vietnam is true. At times they were not much more than a mob. I would spend my last days in Vietnam taking bunkers apart and putting them back together.

I met another Marine lieutenant on his last days, too. Pete Waldinger was from Boston, a Harvard man. Pete played ice hockey back in the World. We were both short-timers, we had both seen too much waste and stupidity, and we both had tough attitudes about finishing our tours and getting out. It was too late to be killed now.

The army at this firebase had made a silent pact with the enemy: We don't want to be here anyway, so we won't bother you if you don't bother us. The soldiers had a habit of sleeping in the village with the women there. At the time, the idea of closing my eyes in the same room with a local made the hair on my neck stand up.

The enemy did not like the new deal with the Marines. The rifle battalion sent ahead of us to defend the firebase was my old battalion, 3/7, although Captain Van Riper and almost all the rest had either rotated or taken a hit.

It did not go well here for 3/7, either. Because the army did not patrol the area, the NVA had taken advantage and built a complex fighting position with reinforced bunkers, trenches, tunnels, and spider holes. One of 3/7's early patrols walked six hundred meters off the hill and into an ambush. The rest of the platoon, then the rest of the company, then the rest of the battalion got involved before it was over. I heard the battalion suffered fifty casualties with more than a dozen dead, including the battalion commander.

As for us, the enemy dropped incoming on us every other night. They had a couple of large mortars and a large recoilless rifle for which they seemed to have plenty of ammunition. Pete and I took turns on duty as fire direction officer. One of us slept in the FDC and the other slept in the bunker we shared. We were terribly vulnerable. The wire came right up to the door of our bunker, and our lines were very thin. As it happened, my nights on duty were usually the nights we took incoming.

One morning, the 175 platoon's XO stopped me and said, "We are having a formation in a few minutes. We are going to present awards and you need to fall in up front."

Thirty minutes later we had a formation, and our major, the platoon commander, introduced the 11th Marines regimental commander. The full colonel told us how happy he was to be with us. Then he read a service citation for one of the FDC members. The award related to the planning of fires for some named operation. Next he called my name. I had no idea what was coming. I was thinking, "This should be interesting. At least it's not a court-martial."

The colonel began to read:

For heroic achievement in connection with combat operations against the enemy in the Republic of Vietnam while serving as a Forward Air Controller with Company B, 1st Battalion, 5th Marines, 1st Marine Division. On the afternoon of 9 June 1969, Company B was moving toward the battalion command post when the Marines came under intense small-arms and automatic-weapons fire from a North Vietnamese Army unit entrenched in the village of An Bong, near the An Hoa Combat Base. Upon contact, the Marines sustained several casualties, many of whom required medical evacuation. Reacting instantly, First Lieutenant Hardwick requested a medical evacuation helicopter and then directed his men to establish a landing zone. When the company command post came under fire, he quickly maneuvered to an advantageous position from which to direct the fire of supporting helicopter gunships upon the hostile positions. As he controlled the aircraft, he simultaneously rendered first aid to two wounded Marines. The medical evacuation aircraft arrived and were unable to land due to the heavy volume of enemy fire directed at the landing zone. First Lieutenant Hardwick rapidly selected a more secure landing area and then supervised the movement of the injured Marines to the aircraft, personally carrying several of the casualties across an open rice paddy while under hostile fire. When the Marines launched an assault upon the enemy positions, First Lieutenant Hardwick skillfully directed gunship fire upon the hostile targets to within ten meters of the friendly position. His heroic and timely actions contributed significantly to the Marines being able to overrun the enemy fortifications and to the air strikes accounting for twenty hostile soldiers killed.

First Lieutenant Hardwick's courage, superb leadership, and unwavering devotion to duty in the face of great personal danger were in keeping with the highest traditions of the Marine Corps and of the United States Naval Service.

When he had finished reading, he pinned a Bronze Star with combat V (for valor) on my blouse and said, "That reads very nicely."

I felt very proud, but you could have knocked me over

with a feather. The entire unit had performed many truly courageous acts that day. All I did was direct the gunships and get the wounded out. All I did was my job. I did not feel that my actions had earned a medal, and after Liberty Bridge I had developed a cynical attitude about medals. But on that day, with the entire battery standing by, I would take it. Today it is one of my proudest possessions and hangs in my office next to my saber.

I gained tremendous face within the gun platoon. Most of these 0800s would fight their entire war from a bunker, behind the wire. It was still a war, and you could still get killed, but their war was charts and radios and gun pits. Most would never actually fight the enemy in combat. Suddenly everyone in the platoon knew my name. I went from being just another surly short-timer with an attitude to Stud Duck.

Several enlisted men stopped by and introduced themselves. One young Marine heard I was from Oklahoma and came by to tell me that he was, too. He had been in-country for three weeks, and I guess talking to me helped him believe that his time might also pass. The count was down to twenty-seven days. Come on, twenty-six!

It is midafternoon. I am in the FDC when suddenly we begin to take incoming. They had never hit us in daytime, but nothing surprises me at this point. The entrance to the FDC is at the bottom of a thirty-meter slope. The bunker is surrounded by giant boulders. At the top of the slope are the hooches, the gun pits, and the rest of the platoon. The first detonation causes a lot of yelling up on top. I stick my head out and see the major. He had been standing near a jeep with two other Marines when the first round hit. It knocked the two Marines down, and the major is trying to get someone to come and help him. I start up the slope just as one of the next rounds impacts in the rocks overhead and blasts rock and hot shrapnel down around me. I take only ten or twelve steps when those icy steel fingers make a fist around my intestines.

My old friend terror is back. I find myself stuck between strides, with my stomach knotted tight. Several Marines show up to help the major, and I turn slowly around, push myself into the upright position, and walk stiffly back into the FDC. My tour has gone full circle. My mind has slipped into survival mode. I am beginning to believe that I might make it. I will be no good to fight anymore, unless I absolutely have to.

Six days later the count is down to twenty-one days. Come on, twenty! I am on duty in the FDC. It is past midnight, and I am asleep when the first round hits. It hits the FDC bunker itself, and dirt, dust, and the acrid smell of the explosion immediately fill the room. I jump to my feet as other Marines also scramble up. The enemy often launches ground attacks against artillery units under the mask of incoming. The procedure for us is the same, send front and rear security out to protect our bunker access, and hang tight.

We cannot depress the muzzles of our 175s low enough to fire at close targets, so we must rely on the infantry and the 105mm battery to defend us. I move through the settling dust to the chart table. I send one Marine out the back for rear security. My Okie is standing by the front door with his rifle. I say, "Okay, you take the front." He never looks or listens. I have told him to go, and he just bolts out the front door.

Inside, we all hear it coming. There is no time to even yell to him. He takes off, we hear it coming, and he runs right into the next round. When it detonates, we hear an immediate scream. "I'm hit! Oh God, help me! Lieutenant!"

I run to the blast wall and stop. I do not want to go outside with enemy ordnance raining down. I look over my shoulder at the room, and the whole room is looking right back at me. I press my body against the blast wall. My mind's eye can read the telegram. "Dear Mrs. Hardwick stop Just 21 more days stop He almost made it stop Damn stop."

The next round is long. I bolt around the blast wall and run into the darkness.

He is only fifteen or twenty feet outside the door, and in the darkness I run right into him, stumble, and fall on top of him. Through the pain and the darkness he wraps his arms around my legs and clamps down tight. I find myself trapped. My head is down and my butt is up. He has my legs clinched down tight. I cannot budge.

I can tell by how loudly he is screaming and the strength in his arms that he is in more pain than danger. But struggle as I can, I am not able to get free enough to help either one of us. I fight back the urge to panic. The next round is coming and the thought flashes through my mind to draw my pistol and either beat him with it or shoot him. I must get free. The round hits high in the rocks and scatters rock and shrapnel down on us. Suddenly he lets go. I roll to one side, grab him under his arms, and begin to drag him back toward the bunker. We are nearly there when my boots slip and I fall down.

For the second time in my tour, Marines grab me by my flak jacket and jerk me up off the ground. I manage to hold on to the Okie, and the four of us come rolling backward behind the blast wall in a thrashing, screaming pile.

More Marines grab at us, and a corpsman pulls the Okie up on a table. We tear open his shirt and rip open his trousers. He has a dozen puncture wounds on the lower half of his torso and down his legs to his knees. The two most serious wounds are at the right knee, one of them through the kneecap. His penis has been nicked and has a divot missing. Like all soldiers, he worries first about his manhood.

I look up at another Marine. I say, "Take the front." He looks at me with big eyes. Then without comment, he goes to the blast wall, listens, and disappears into the darkness.

We shoot the Okie full of morphine, and when we're sure the incoming has stopped, we make a litter and transfer him to the infirmary. At first light he will go to Da Nang.

I turn my cot on its side and kick the dirt and dust from it. I lie down and go back to sleep.

October 15, 1969. The count is down to twelve days. I had just sat down with my breakfast when the battery XO walked past behind me. He stopped and quietly said, "Your orders came in. You're going home." My heart skipped.

I said, "That's great. When do I go?" And he said, "This morning. Get your gear and catch the nine o'clock bird." I wanted to yell, I wanted to scream, I wanted to throw a chair, I wanted to *do* something. Instead, I sat quietly for a moment to feel the feeling that I was going home. It was almost 0800 when I found Pete to tell him I was "gone." I wished him luck, grabbed my gear, and waited at the LZ until the chopper heading for Da Nang arrived.

When I got to 11th Marines, John Juracek was already there. Our flight to Okinawa was the next afternoon. We went to a movie but spent most of the evening just enjoying the feeling of being alive. The next morning at breakfast, we ran into two gold bars (two new second lieutenants) who discovered we were headed home and stopped us to chat.

Enough troops had been withdrawn that the course of the war had become obvious to everyone. Marines who had arrived just after John and I had already been pulled out in one move and boarded ships to begin the two-week ocean trip to San Diego.

Now every new soldier and Marine going into combat knew that he was going into a fight that we were quitting.

These two new guys had been issued jungle boots and utilities just the afternoon before. They were looking at what might be twelve-month tours, or even less. They would meet 11th Marines' regimental commander today, and he was going to give them a choice. The Marine Corps had plenty of platoon commanders. In fact, the casualty rate had slowed, and new officers were plentiful. They could go to the field as FOs, or stay at 11th Marines and be sent to a battery somewhere.

For one of them, there was no question. "Forget it." He was plain. "The war is ending, we are already pulling out. It would be crazy for anyone to take the chance now, to step on a land mine."

The other new officer was ambivalent. "I worry about the mines. . . ." He hesitated. "I joined to fight . . . I want to be in a fight . . . but if you go out, you could hit a mine." It may be telling that neither officer ever mentioned being shot. He asked some questions about the mines, and we told him he was right to worry.

Young Americans would fight, and fight hard, for another twenty-four months. More than twelve thousand would die; thousands and thousands more would be maimed or incapacitated.

All John and I wanted was out.

That afternoon we checked our gear and boarded a chartered jet. As the plane lifted off and began to turn north and east toward Okinawa, I knew that if we looked back out the window, we would see fighter aircraft making loops through the atmosphere toward an unseen enemy below. Neither of us chose to look back. The enemy had been shooting at us when we arrived, we fought as hard as we could for most of thirteen months, and they were still shooting at us when we left. All John and I wanted was out.

Postscript

We stayed three days in Okinawa, and when we reached San Francisco we split up. I headed for Texas and took a twenty-day leave. Just before Thanksgiving 1969, I reported to Camp Lejeune in Jacksonville, North Carolina. By coincidence, I had thirteen months left on a three-year commitment to the Marines.

So many Marines were returning from Vietnam at that point that on-base housing was unavailable. We found a house in town and managed to move our belongings. That night, as I drove to the base to present my orders, the radio was full of the My Lai massacre and the army's Lt. William Calley.

I found it a bitter irony. After the courage and resolution I had seen expressed on all sides of the war, the world's single lasting memory of the war in Vietnam would be My Lai. And bitter would have been the best word to describe my feelings. Angry and bitter. War is always wasteful. This one, especially so.

In February, I was shipped to Guantánamo Bay, Cuba, on temporary assignment. I had to leave my family again, this time for five months.

Jim Harvey was in Cuba when I arrived. Guantánamo was really laid back. Almost everyone there was straight back from the war and just doing time until they could get out. For five months we lifted weights, played tennis, jogged in the hills, and drank. I finally learned to like country music.

Vietnam was the one subject that was not mentioned. Some of the guys were very sensitive about it. Jim would not allow the subject, in any form.

Word came down that the Corps was bumping its manpower limits. The casualty rate was still slowing. A six-month early-out was offered to interested first lieutenants. There was, of course, a stampede. I was surprised by some of the individuals who stayed, but most of us never would have joined had there not been a war, and most of us just wanted out.

I was processed back to civilian life about June 5, 1970. For the fifth time in three years, we packed up our belongings and moved.

Being a civilian was a strange sensation. By the time I got back to the World, I could walk in the grass without worrying about mines. I noticed in Cuba that I still had the revulsion to yellow smoke. The trigger response was still there, but the overall response had significantly faded. In time it would *all* fade.

For the first two or three years, every day was the anniversary of a name, or a face, or some place. For ten years I tried hard to stop thinking about it.

After twenty-two years I would finally drink apple juice again. I have still never eaten fruit cocktail from a can since, but in the land of the giant supermarket, who needs to?

When I was discharged, I first went to Dallas to look

for a job, but in the summer of 1970, Collins Radio and Ling-Temco-Vought had both just done giant belly flops and they, along with several other big companies, were filling the streets with newly unemployed. I spent a week dropping my résumé on "the pile." I was calling friends to get ideas. Someone suggested Houston.

A cousin who lived in Houston helped me set up several interviews, and I found myself on Interstate 45 headed south. Driving into town, I saw the skyline and began to sense a kind of electricity in the air. The traffic was fast, and business was fast; you could feel an excitement. Before I had stopped at the first stoplight, I had fallen in love with the place.

July 10, 1970. All three of the interviews went well and I called my wife to tell her we would be landing in Houston. I felt that one of the three companies would offer me a job. And sure enough, when I went back to my first choice, I was shown into the office of one of the partners. They were doing very well in a very competitive market. He was a good guy. Quite bright.

He offered me coffee and he talked about the company's plans for the future. Then he said, "We pride ourselves in taking only the very best people available. We think that is you. We would like you to join us here and help us make this future come true . . . and, Bill, let me say something else . . . if you decide to join us here, the fact that you went to Vietnam would absolutely *not* count against you. We take only the best, but once you are here, everyone starts out as an equal. No one here will care about where you've been. I doubt if anyone here would ever even mention it."

He was trying to be kind and to reassure me, and I was not offended. It was just the times. Besides, they had

a good deal going and they were making money. So I
took the job.

The partner clapped his hands and said emphatically,
"Terrific! In that case, let's go to lunch. We'll take Jim
Corbitt with us. Jim will be important for your getting
started here. He not only has all the marketing and de-
mographic information, he will help you with your sales
presentations. He is also our liaison for all governmen-
tal agencies. Why, you and Jim will be good buddies in
no time at all."

Good buddies!

I choked a laugh that sounded more like a snort and
felt myself begin to blush. The partner was getting his
coat and gave me a big-brother kind of smile at the joke
he didn't catch.

"Good buddies," I said and clapped my hands. "Terrific, I can't wait." And then we both laughed.

> War . . . huh. What is it good for?
> Absolutely nothing. Say it again, child.
> —EDWIN STARR, "War"

For the epilogue, see the website www.downsouthvietnam.
com